What Price the Moral High Ground?

ROBERT H. FRANK

Princeton University Press   Princeton and Oxford

What Price the Moral High Ground?

How to Succeed without Selling Your Soul

Copyright © 2004 by Princeton University Press
Published by Princeton University Press,
41 William Street, Princeton, New Jersey 08540
In the United Kingdom: Princeton University Press,
6 Oxford Street, Woodstock, Oxfordshire OX20 1TW
press.princeton.edu

First printing, 2004
Paperback reissue, 2010
ISBN: 978-0-691-14694-2
Library of Congress Control Number 2009941950

British Library Cataloging-in-Publication Data is available

This book has been composed in Electra

Printed on acid-free paper. ∞

Printed in the United States of America

10 9 8 7 6 5 4 3 2 1

Contents

Introduction
Infectious Good

WITH REVELATIONS OF corporate accounting scandals dominating the news in the summer of 2002, United States Federal Reserve Chairman Alan Greenspan told a Senate banking committee in Washington that leaders of America's business community appeared to be in the grip of "infectious greed." The problem, in his view, was "not that humans have become any more greedy than in generations past," but rather that "the avenues to express greed have grown so enormously."

Many saw the scandals as confirming the cynical view that *doing well* (successfully pursuing one's narrow self-interest) is accomplished entirely at the expense of *doing good* (respecting the legitimate interests of others, even when no one is looking). As conventionally taught, both economic theory and evolutionary psychology are not only consistent with this view, but also provide intellectual ammunition for it. The argument, in brief, is that while the world might indeed be a better place if people restrained themselves for the common good, competitive pressures make it naïve to expect that anyone will do so.

The notion of contagion figures prominently in this argument. Most citizens, for example, recognize the need for the government to collect taxes to finance public services, and are prepared to do their part. Yet experience has shown that vigorous enforcement measures are necessary to maintain high rates of tax compliance. If it becomes known that people can claim questionable tax exemptions without penalty, many will do so, and their actions inevitably pressure others to respond in kind. Over time, the standards that define acceptable conduct shift. This dynamic surely played an important part in the recent corporate accounting scandals. Accounting practices that would have seemed beyond the pale in an earlier environment came to be viewed as acceptable once they became more commonplace.

Both economic theory and evolutionary theory, as historically taught, encourage the hard-nosed view that the only way to sustain pro-social behavior is through strict rules and sanctions. *Homo economicus* does not return a stranger's wallet if he finds it on a street corner; nor does he make anonymous donations to charity; nor does he vote in presidential elections; nor does he leave tips when dining in a restaurant he does not expect to visit again. By the same token, the stereotypical Darwinian actor does not help a victim in distress unless that victim is likely to return the favor or is a sufficiently close genetic relative. The expectation encouraged by these theories is that people are willing to make sacrifices for the common good only if society can confront them with significant penalties when they fail to do so.

This expectation is almost certainly incorrect. Indeed, recent theoretical and empirical insights in both economics and biology suggest a more nuanced view. On the empirical front, there is persuasive evidence that in many situations we simply do not behave in the narrowly self-interested ways predicted by traditional theories. We usually leave tips when dining on the road, for example, and millions of us vote in presidential elections. Most of us incur avoidable costs in these and a host of other situations in which we could behave opportunistically with no possibility of penalty. On the theoretical front, we are now poised to understand why being predisposed to incur such costs need not entail significant penalties, even in the bitterly competitive environments thought to be most hostile to this posture.

In the essays in this volume, I summarize a variety of arguments and evidence that bear on the spontaneous emergence of pro-social behavior. The better we are able to appreciate how such behavior can emerge independently of external rewards and sanctions, the better we will be able to shape institutions that encourage desired outcomes, and the better we will be able to sidestep the institutional design disasters that have plagued us in recent years.

The essays in part I ("Doing Well") lay out the basic argument and evidence for the proposition that people who are intrinsically motivated to adhere to ethical norms often prosper in competitive environments. Chapter 1 ("Forging Commitments That Sustain Cooperation") introduces the paradoxical idea that people can often promote their own narrow ends more effectively by abandoning the direct pursuit of self-interest. This idea is a special case of the broader notion that people can often improve their lot by making commitments that foreclose valuable options — as, for example, when someone believed to be scrupulously honest is for that reason promoted to fill an important, well-paying job that entails strong temptations to cheat.

For an honest person to be favored in this way, it is necessary that others be able to make accurate assessments about his or her character. The obvious difficulty is that the rewards for successful mimicry are often enormous. If there are gains from being honest, there would be even larger gains from merely appearing to be honest. In chapter 2 ("Can Cooperators Find One Another?") I report the results of experiments conducted in collaboration with my Cornell colleagues Tom Gilovich and Dennis Regan in which subjects were given a risk-free opportunity to earn more money by cheating their partner in a simple game. Contrary to the predictions of traditional models, almost 75 percent did not avail themselves of this opportunity; and more important, those subjects who predicted their partners would cheat were correct at more than twice chance accuracy rates.

Chapter 3 ("Adaptive Rationality and the Moral Emotions") applies arguments and evidence from the first two chapters to the timeless question of how morality and rationality are related. The rational choice models employed by many contemporary social scientists treat narrow self-interest as the only important human motive. Scholars in this tradition see a fundamental disconnect between rationality and morality. They view society's attempts to articulate and enforce moral norms as attempts to avoid the losses inherent in social dilemmas — situations in which the rational pursuit of individual self-interest leads to outcomes that are undesirable from the perspective of larger groups. Chapter 3 suggests the possibility of a much closer link between rationality and morality. Without claiming the two concepts are identical, it suggests that a rational individual will often be unlikely to achieve his material ends if the moral emotions are missing from his character.

Many economists and business ethicists point out that because firms are not people, it is a mistake to expect them to adhere to moral norms like the ones that govern interpersonal relations. Yet firms are owned by people, managed by people, and staffed by people. In chapter 4 ("Can Socially Responsible Firms Survive in Competitive Environments?") I suggest that we cannot expect people to be guided by their moral emotions in their personal dealings with others and then act independently of those same emotions when they go to work. Firms confront many of the same kinds of social dilemmas that ordinary people do. Purely self-interested persons often cannot make the kinds of commitments necessary to solve these dilemmas, and it turns out that the same is true of purely self-interested firms. Chapter 4 discusses a variety of separate mechanisms whereby a firm that incurs additional costs in going beyond what is required by law is nonetheless able to prosper in competition with more opportunistic rivals.

The chapters in part II ("Doing Good") address the question of how much people are willing to sacrifice in the name of their ethical concerns. Chapter 5 ("What Price the Moral High Ground?") employs the economist's time-honored method of inferring strength of preference from patterns of compensating wage differentials in the labor market. Economists attempt to gauge the value of workplace safety, for example, by examining how much more people get paid in risky jobs than in relatively safe ones. In the same fashion, chapter 5 attempts to assess the strength of pro-social motivations by examining the wage premium for performing morally suspect tasks (such as testifying before Congress that exposure to secondhand smoke has not been proved to cause illness). When it comes to explaining why some people earn more than others, even crude measures of employer and occupational moral merit have far more power than traditional economic wage determinants like education, training, and experience.

Traditional economic theory holds that wages within a firm will closely track individual employee contributions to the firm's bottom line. Yet in virtually every firm, individual wages vary far less than individual productivity. Chapter 6 ("Local Status, Fairness, and Wage Compression Revisited") suggests that one reason for the apparent contradiction is that workers care not only about how much they earn in absolute terms, as assumed by traditional models, but also about how their salaries compare with those of their co-workers. But although most workers might like to occupy a high-ranking position vis-à-vis their co-workers, it is a mathematical constraint that exactly half the members of any group be in the bottom half. Chapter 6 describes an intra-firm theory of justice according to which workers can enjoy a high-ranking position vis-à-vis their co-workers only if they are willing, in effect, to share a substantial share of their pay with them.

Another nettlesome observation confronting proponents of traditional self-interest models is the fact that Americans donate more than $200 billion each year to various charities, many of them anonymously. Chapter 7 ("Motivation, Cognition, and Charitable Giving") argues that to explain the observed patterns of giving, we must not only abandon the narrow self-interest assumption, but we must also relax the assumption that individuals are always cognitively efficient in pursuit of their goals. Any charity whose potential donor base consisted only of homo-economicus stereotypes would quickly be forced to close its doors. Chapter 7 examines the fundraising task of a charity confronting potential donors who more closely resemble real persons — people who are narrowly selfish in some of their attitudes, pro-social in others, and who make occasional mistakes even when the problems before them are relatively simple.

The chapters in part III ("Forging Better Outcomes") advance the claim that while moral behavior can emerge spontaneously in competitive environments, the way we structure those environments strongly affects the amount of moral behavior we actually observe. Chapter 8 ("Social Norms as Positional Arms-Control Agreements") suggests that although most of us appear to be born equipped with brain circuitry that enables us to experience sympathy, guilt, and other moral emotions, the specific conditions under which we experience these emotions and the specific ways in which they constrain our behavior are highly context-dependent. The prospect of guilt is known to summon self-restraint across a variety of cultural settings, for example, but the specific behaviors that give rise to guilt may be very different for a mafia captain than for an Episcopal bishop. This chapter argues that the particular social norms that a group seeks to enforce depends on the social dilemmas that figure most prominently in its local environment. It suggests that numerous specific social norms in American culture function to curb positional arms races — patterns of mutually offsetting expenditure escalation by rivals competing for important resources.

Just as norms have a powerful effect on behavior, so, too, do theories of behavior themselves. In chapter 9 ("Does Studying Economics Inhibit Cooperation?") I report the results of a study conducted with Tom Gilovich and Dennis Regan, in which we found that the traditional self-interest model has important implications for the choices people make in social dilemmas. We found, in particular, that the likelihood of making selfish choices in such dilemmas rose sharply with people's exposure to training in economics. In light of the arguments and evidence presented in part I, the irony of this finding is that the ultimate victims of opportunistic behavior are often the very people who practice it.

Because there are obvious limits to the ability of laws and norms to regulate human behavior, it is an encouraging prospect that pro-social behavior can emerge spontaneously and become self-sustaining. Yet the mere fact that people can be good in the absence of external rewards and sanctions provides no reason to think that laws, norms, and regulations are unnecessary. In the Epilogue ("The Importance of Sanctions") I caution against thinking that we need not ferret out and punish wrongdoers aggressively. With respect to tax evasion, for example, although the United States has enjoyed the highest degree of tax compliance among large developed countries, we cannot hope to continue that status if we continue to cut the staff and budget of the IRS sharply. Context matters. Good behavior is contagious, but so, too, is bad behavior. An overriding emphasis on voluntary compliance is bad public policy, not just because it requires those who comply voluntarily to pay an unfair share, but also because it inevitably generates a race to the bottom.

Part I

Doing Well

1

Forging Commitments That Sustain Cooperation

RATIONAL CHOICE MODELS typically assume that people choose among possible actions so as to maximize the extent to which they achieve their goals. Such models yield few interesting predictions, however, without first introducing specific assumptions about the nature of those goals. How can we predict what someone will do unless we first have some idea of what he or she cares about?

The most frequent move at this step is to assume that people pursue goals that are self-interested in fairly narrow terms. Yet many common actions appear to be at odds with this assumption. We leave tips at out-of-town restaurants we will never visit again. We donate bone marrow in an effort to save the lives of perfect strangers. We find wallets and return them with the cash intact. We vote in presidential elections.

People uncomfortable with the self-interest assumption often respond to such contradictions by assuming a broader range of human objectives. Tips in out of town restaurants? We leave them because we care not only about our personal wealth, but also about holding up our end of an implicit understanding with the server. Voting in presidential elections? We do it because we care about fulfilling our civic duty. And so on.

The problem with this approach, however, is that if analysts are totally unconstrained in terms of the number of goals they can attribute to people, virtually any behavior can be "explained" after the fact simply by positing a taste for it. As students of the scientific method are quick to emphasize, a theory that can explain everything ends up explaining nothing at all. To be scientifically valuable, a theory must make predictions that are at least in principle capable of being falsified.

And hence the dilemma confronting proponents of rational choice theory: versions that assume narrow self-interest are clearly not descriptive, whereas those to which goals can be added without constraint lack real explanatory power. Yes, people seem to get a warm glow from giving to charity. But why does that give them a warm glow? Why don't they get a warm glow from *not* giving to charity, since they'll end up with more money for their own purposes that way, and since the absence of any individual's gift will make no perceptible difference?

Evolutionary psychology offers a principled way of resolving this dilemma. Instead of making essentially arbitrary assumptions about people's goals, it views our goals not as ends in themselves, but rather as means in our struggle to acquire the resources needed to survive and reproduce. At first glance it might appear that a Darwinian approach to the study of human motivation would be strongly biased toward a narrow view of self-interest. Certainly, best-selling titles such as *The Selfish Gene* and *The Moral Animal* have done little to dispel that view. Yet Darwinian analysis also suggests mechanisms that might support a considerably broader conception of human motivation. And because of its inherent bias in favor of self-interest, the Darwinian framework constitutes a conservative standard by which to judge whether a specific goal can be added to the analyst's list. Thus, according to this framework, a goal can be added only if a plausible account can be offered of why pursuit of that goal is consistent with survival under competitive conditions.

The specific idea I explore here has a distinctly paradoxical flavor. It is that people can often promote their own narrow ends more effectively by pursuing certain goals that are in clear conflict with self-interest. This idea is a special case of the broader notion that people can often improve their lot by making commitments that foreclose valuable options.

The most vivid illustration remains an early example offered by Thomas Schelling (1960), who described a kidnapper who suddenly gets cold feet. He wants to set his victim free, but is afraid the victim will go to the police. In return for his freedom, the victim gladly promises not to do so. The problem, however, is that both realize it will no longer be in the victim's interest to keep this promise once he is free. And so the kidnapper reluctantly concludes that he must kill the victim.

The kidnapper and his victim confront a commitment problem, and to solve it they need a commitment device, something that gives the victim an incentive to keep his promise. Schelling suggests the following way out (1960, 43–44): "If the victim has committed an act whose disclosure could lead to blackmail, he may confess it; if not, he might commit one in the presence of his captor, to create a bond that will ensure his silence." Keeping his promise will still be unpleasant for the victim once he is freed, but clearly less so than not being able to make a credible promise in the first place.

In Schelling's example, the blackmailable offense is an effective commitment device because it changes the victim's material incentives in the desired way. Is it also possible to solve commitment problems by means of less tangible changes in incentives? Can moral emotions, for example, function as commitment devices? And, if so, what evidence might persuade a skeptic that natural selection had favored such emotions at least in part for that reason? These questions are my focus in this chapter.

A first step in trying to answer them will be to adopt a common language. In what follows I will use the term "contractual commitments" to describe commitments facilitated by contracts (formal or informal) that alter material incentives. Schelling's parable is an example of contractual commitment. I will use the term "emotional commitments" to describe commitments facilitated by emotions.

Two Examples

What kinds of problems are contractual commitments and emotional commitments meant to solve? I will discuss two illustrative examples. The first is a commitment problem typically solved by legal contracts, while the second is one for which such contracts are not quite up to the task.

Consider first the problem of searching for an apartment. You have just moved to a new city, and you need a place to live. If you are in Los Angeles or some other metropolis, you cannot possibly inspect each of the thousands of vacant apartments, so you check the listings and visit a few to get a rough idea of what is available — the range of prices, amenities, locations, and other features you care about. As your search proceeds, you find a unit that seems unusually attractive on the basis of your impressions of the relevant distributions. You want to close the deal. At that point, you *know* there is a better apartment out there somewhere, but your time is too valuable to justify looking further. You want to get on with your life.

Having made that decision, the next important step is to make a commitment with the owner of the apartment. You do not want to move in and then a month later be told to leave. After all, by then you will have bought curtains, hung your art, installed phone and cable service, and so on. If you are forced to leave, not only will those investments be for naught, but you will also have to begin searching anew for a place to live.

The landlord also has an interest in seeing you stay for an extended period, since he, too, went to a lot of trouble and expense to rent the apartment. He advertised it and showed it to dozens of other prospective tenants, none of whom seemed quite as stable and trustworthy as you seemed to be.

The upshot is that even though you know there is a better apartment out there, and even though your landlord knows that a better tenant will eventually come along, you both have a strong interest in committing yourselves to ignore such opportunities. The standard solution is to sign a formal lease—a contractual commitment that prevents each of you from accepting other offers that might later prove attractive. If you move out, you must still pay your rent for the duration of the lease. If your landlord asks you to leave, the lease empowers you to refuse.

The ability to commit by signing a lease raises the amount a tenant would be willing to pay for any given apartment, and reduces the amount that its owner would be willing to accept. Without the security provided by this contractual commitment, many valuable exchanges would not occur. Leases foreclose valuable options, to be sure. But that is exactly what the signatories want them to do.

The person searching for a mate confronts an essentially similar commitment problem. You want a mate, but not just any old mate. In the hope of meeting that special someone, you accept additional social invitations and make other efforts to expand your circle of friends. After dating for a while, you feel you know a fair amount about what kinds of people are out there—what sorts of dispositions they have, their ethical values, their attitudes toward children, their cultural and recreational interests, their social and professional skills, and so on. Among the people you meet, you are drawn to one in particular. Your luck holds, and that person feels the same way about you. You both want to move forward and start investing in your relationship. You want to get married, buy a house, have children. Few of these investments make sense, however, unless you both expect your relationship to continue for an extended period.

But what if something goes wrong? No matter what your mate's vision of the ideal partner may be, you know there's someone out there who comes closer to that ideal than you. What if that someone suddenly shows up? Or what if one of you falls seriously ill? Just as landlords and tenants can gain by committing themselves, partners in marriage have a similar interest in foreclosing future options.

The marriage contract is one way of attempting to achieve the desired commitment. On reflection, however, we see that a legal contract is not particularly well-suited for creating the kind of commitment both parties want in this situation. Even fiercely draconian legal sanctions can at most force people to remain with spouses they would prefer to leave. But marriage on those terms hardly serves the goals each partner had originally hoped to achieve.

A far more secure commitment results if the legal contract is reinforced by emotional bonds of affection. The plain fact is that many relationships are not threatened when a new potential partner who is kinder, wealthier, more charming, and better looking comes along. Someone who has become deeply emotionally attached to his or her spouse often does not *want* to pursue new opportunities, even ones that, in purely objective terms, might seem more promising.

That is not to say that emotional commitments are fail-safe. Who among us would not experience at least mild concern upon hearing that his wife was having dinner with Ralph Fiennes this evening, or that her husband was having a drink with Gwyneth Paltrow? Yet even imperfect emotional commitments free most couples from such concerns most of the time.

Again, the important point is that even though emotional commitments foreclose potentially valuable opportunities, they also confer important benefits. An emotional commitment to one's spouse is valuable in the coldly rational Darwinian cost-benefit calculus because it promotes investments that enhance reproductive fitness. But note the ironic twist. These commitments work best when they deflect people from thinking explicitly about their spousal relationships in cost-benefit terms. People who consciously approach those relationships with scorecards in hand are much less satisfied with their marriages than others; and when therapists try to get people to think in cost-benefit terms about their relationships, it often seems to backfire (Murstein, Cerreto, and Mac-Donald 1977). That may just not be the way we're *meant* to think about close personal relationships.

Sustainable Cooperation

Solving commitment problems is important not only for successful pair bonding, but also for achieving a variety of other forms of cooperation. Indeed, the prisoner's dilemma — the ubiquitous metaphor for the difficulty of achieving cooperation among rational, self-interested individuals — is in essence a simple commitment problem. Both players in a prisoner's dilemma get higher payoffs when both cooperate than when both defect, yet no matter which choice one player makes, the other can get a still higher payoff by defecting. When each player defects, however, each receives a lower payoff than if both had cooperated, and hence the dilemma. Each player would be happy to join a mutual commitment to cooperate if he could. But when such commitments cannot be made, the dominant strategy is to defect.

The metaphor is a powerful one. It helps to explain the generally pessimistic tone of evolutionary biologists who have written on the subject of altruism and cooperation. Consider a population consisting of two distinct types of people, cooperators and defectors, who earn their living by interacting with one another in a game whose payoffs take the form of a prisoner's dilemma. When interacting with others, cooperators always cooperate and defectors always defect. Both types do best when they interact with cooperators. But if the two types looked exactly the same, they would interact with other individuals at random. And because defection is the dominant strategy in the prisoner's dilemma, defectors would always receive a higher expected payoff than cooperators in these random interactions. By virtue of their higher payoffs, defectors would eventually drive cooperators to extinction — and hence the standard result in behavioral biology that genuine cooperation or altruism cannot survive in competitive environments.

If the same individuals face a prisoner's dilemma repeatedly, cooperation can often be sustained, because individuals will have future opportunities to retaliate against those who defect in the current round (Rapoport and Chammah 1965; Trivers 1971; Axelrod and Hamilton 1981; and Axelrod 1984). But although cooperation motivated by threat of punishment is surely better than none at all, such behavior does not really capture what we mean by genuine cooperation. When cooperative play is favored by ordinary material incentives, as when interactions are repeated, it is more aptly called prudence than cooperation.

Writers in the standard tradition seem to agree that universal defection is the expected outcome in prisoner's dilemmas that are not repeated. Yet examples abound in which people cooperate in one-shot prisoner's dilemmas. Waiters usually provide good service in restaurants located on interstate highways, and diners in those restaurants usually leave the expected tip at meal's end, even though both realize they are unlikely ever to see each other again. People return wallets they find on street corners, often anonymously, and usually with the cash intact. Millions of people brave long lines and unpleasant November weather to vote in presidential elections, even though they know their individual votes will not be decisive, even in a contest as close as the one for Florida's twenty-five electoral votes in 2000.

The pessimistic conclusion that genuine cooperation is impossible would be reversed completely if cooperators and defectors could somehow be distinguished from one another at a glance. Suppose, for example, that cooperators had a birthmark on their foreheads in the form of a red C, and that defectors had a birthmark in the shape of a red D (or no birthmark at all). Then those with a C on their foreheads could pair off together and reap the higher payoff from mutual cooperation. The defectors would be left to interact with one another. In this situation, the defectors are the ones who would be driven to extinction.

If experience is any guide, however, this optimistic conclusion is also flawed. Although millions of public radio listeners make generous contributions to support the programming they enjoy, substantially larger numbers take a free ride. And at least some people keep the cash in the wallets they find on city sidewalks.

To describe the mixture of motives and behavior we actually observe, we need an intermediate model, one in which cooperators and defectors are observably different in some way, but not transparently so. We may have some idea of whether a specific individual is likely to cooperate in the prisoner's dilemma, but we cannot be sure.

As Adam Smith and David Hume realized, the emotion of sympathy is a good candidate for the moral sentiment that motivates cooperation in social dilemmas. Your goal as an individual is to interact with someone who feels sympathy for your interests, in the hope that such a person will be internally motivated to cooperate, even though he could earn more by defecting.

But how do you know whether someone feels sympathy for your interests? Darwin (1965 [1872]) wrote of the hard-wired link between emotional states in the brain and various details of involuntary facial expression and body language. Consider the crude drawing shown in figure 1.1. This drawing shows only a few details, yet people in every culture recognize even this simple abstraction as an expression of sadness, distress, sympathy, or some other closely related emotion. Most people cannot produce this expression on command (Ekman 1985). (Sit in front of a mirror and try it!) Yet the muscles of the human face create the expression automatically when the relevant emotion is experienced (Darwin 1965 [1872]). Suppose you stub your toe painfully, leading an acquaintance who witnesses your injury to manifest that expression immediately. Such a person is more likely to be a trustworthy trading partner than someone who reacted to the same incident without expression.

Simple facial expressions, of course, are not the only clues on which we rely, or even the most important ones. In ways I will describe presently, we construct character judgments over extended periods on the basis of a host of other subtle signals, many of which enter only subconscious awareness. On the basis of these impressions, among potential trading partners we choose those we feel are most likely to weigh not just their own interests when deciding what to do, but our own interests as well.

Defectors have an obvious incentive to mimic whatever signs we use

Figure 1.1

for identifying reliable trading partners. Selection pressure should strongly favor capacities for effective deception, and examples of such capacities clearly abound in human interaction. If signals of emotional commitment could be mimicked perfectly and without cost, these signals would eventually cease to be useful. Over time, natural selection would mold false signals into perfect replicas of real ones, driving the capacity for signaling genuine commitment to extinction.

Whether that capacity has been able to stay a step ahead of attempts to mimic it is an issue that is difficult to settle on a priori grounds. Granted, natural selection ought to be good at building a copy of a useful signal. But it also ought to be good at modifying an existing signal to evade mimicry. Which of these opposing tendencies wins out in the end is an empirical question, one to which I devoted considerable attention in my 1988 book, *Passions Within Reason*. There, I also argued that even if we grant the existence of reliable signals of emotional commitment, the resulting equilibrium must entail a mixed population of cooperators and defectors. In any population consisting only of cooperators, no one would be vigilant, and opportunities would thus abound for defectors. In a mixed population, cooperators can survive only by being sufficiently vigilant and skilled in their efforts to avoid good mimics.

Can we, in fact, identify people who are emotionally predisposed to cooperate? My Cornell colleagues Tom Gilovich and Dennis Regan and I (1993b) present evidence from an experimental study that appears to support this possibility. In this study, which I describe in chapter 2, we found that subjects of only brief acquaintance were able to identify defectors with better than twice chance accuracy in a one-shot prisoner's dilemma game. And as the following thought experiment suggests, substantially higher accuracy rates may be possible among people who know one another well:

> Imagine yourself just having returned from a crowded sporting event to discover that you have lost an envelope containing $5000 in cash from your coat pocket. (You had just cashed a check for that amount to pay for a used car you planned to pick up the next morning.) Your name and address were written on the front of the envelope. Can you think of anyone, not related to you by blood or marriage, who you feel certain would return your cash if he or she found it?

Most people say yes. Typically, the persons they name are friends of long duration, choices that seem natural for two reasons. First, the more time one spends with someone else, the more opportunities there are to observe clues to that person's emotional makeup. And second, the more time people spend with a friend, the deeper their emotional bonds are likely to be. Sympathy, affection, and other emotions that motivate trustworthy behavior are likely to be more strongly summoned by interactions with close friends than with perfect strangers.

Notice that, although the people named are usually ones with whom we engage in repeated interactions, the particular episode involving the cash is not a repeated game: keeping the cash would not lead to retaliation in the future because there would be no way of knowing that your friend had found and kept the cash. You are also unlikely to have direct evidence regarding your friend's behavior in similar situations in the past.

When pressed, most people respond that they named the people they did because they felt they knew them well enough to be able to say that they would *want* to return the cash. The prospect of keeping a friend's cash would make them feel so bad that it just wouldn't be worth it.

If you named the people you did for roughly similar reasons, then you accept the central premise of my signaling argument, which is that we can identify (possibly strongly context-dependent) behavioral tendencies such as trustworthiness in at least some other people. That doesn't prove that this premise is correct. But it constitutes a hurdle for those who would persuade us that it is false.

Toward a More Realistic Model

Darwinian models like the ones illustrated in the preceding section are clearly stick-figure caricatures. Although they may capture important features of the reality they attempt to represent, they cannot hope to embody the complex range of human behavior and emotion triggered when individuals have conflicting interests. Yet even such simple models often afford powerful insights.

For precisely this reason, however, we are often prone to interpret them too literally. For example, my stick-figure model encourages us to view people as being either cooperative or not. Under the influence of this model, I once equated the task of solving prisoner's dilemmas to that of finding a trustworthy trading partner. But social psychologists have long been skeptical about the existence of stable individual differences of this sort. They believe that differences in behavior are far more likely to be explained by the details of the situation than by stable differences in individual traits. This insight seems clearly applicable to situations that test our willingness to cooperate. Although individual differences in the overall tendency to cooperate surely do exist, most of us cannot be easily assigned to a single category from the cooperator/defector pair. All but the most extreme sociopaths have within them the capacity to experience sympathy for others and to weigh others' interests when deciding what to do. And although almost all of us have cooperated in situations in which it would have paid to defect, most of us have also let others down on occasion.

The Emergence of Sympathy

I now believe that the search for a reliable trading partner is not a quest to identify an indiscriminately trustworthy individual, but rather a process of creating conditions that make us more likely to elicit cooperative tendencies in one another. In a remarkably insightful essay, David Sally

(2000) has summarized a large literature that bears precisely on this process.

Beginning with the writings of David Hume and Adam Smith, Sally traces the intellectual history of the concept of sympathy and reports on some extremely fascinating results on the mechanics of how it develops in human interactions. I use the term "mechanics" advisedly, for an important thread in the studies he reviews is that we are often remarkably mechanical in the ways we respond to stimuli.

Many of these studies remind me of a behavior that I myself have puzzled over for a long time, which is that I usually set my watch five minutes ahead. Not everyone does this, of course, but I know many who do. We do it because it seems to help us get to appointments on time. But *why*? When someone asks me what time it is, I always report the correct time by simply subtracting five minutes from whatever my watch says. So I am not really fooling myself by setting it ahead. Yet if I have an appointment across campus at 11:00, the mere act of seeing a dial saying 10:55 apparently triggers an emotional reaction in my brain, which in turn gets me going a little more quickly than if I had relied only on my knowledge that the correct time was 10:50. Whatever the details of *how* the actual mechanism works, it clearly does work, as I know from experiments in which I have set my watch to the correct time for extended periods.

Other studies confirm the importance of seemingly mindless physical motions. For example, if you are pulling a lever toward you when an experimenter shows you a Chinese ideograph, you are much more likely than control subjects to give the image a positive evaluation when you are queried about it later. But if you are pushing a lever away from you when you are shown the ideograph, you are much more likely to give it a negative evaluation later (Cacioppo, Priester, and Berntson 1993). If you put a pen between a person's teeth — forcing him to smile, as it were — and then show him a cartoon, he is much more likely to find it funny than if he does not have a pen between his teeth (Strack, Martin, and Stepper 1988).

Similar mechanical stimulus-response patterns are also strongly implicated in the processes by which sympathetic bonds form between people. An important factor in these processes is the concept of valence —

an evaluation that is either positive or negative. Psychologists have identified a universal human tendency to assign an initial valence in response to virtually every category of stimulus — even words that may seem neutral, or photographs, or visual scenes of any kind (Lewin 1935; Bargh 1997).

So, too, with persons. When you meet someone, you make an initial up/down categorization very quickly, probably before you are even consciously aware of it (if indeed you ever become consciously aware of it). Likeness seems to play a role in these judgments (Lazarsfeld and Merton 1954). You are more apt to assign positive valence to someone who is like you in some way — say, in dress, speech patterns, or ethnic background. Reputation matters, as does the character of your initial exchange. Attractiveness is important. Physically attractive persons are far more likely than others to receive a positive initial evaluation (Eagly et al. 1991; Sally, 2000).

Once the initial valence has been assigned, a biased cognitive filter becomes activated. You still evaluate further aspects of your experience with a new acquaintance, but with a slant. If the initial evaluation was positive, you are much more likely to treat ambiguous signals in a positive light. But if your initial impression was negative, you are more likely to assign negative interpretations to those same signals. Such feedback effects often make first impressions far more important than we might like them to be on ethical grounds.

A colleague of mine once described a vivid example of how an initial negative assessment had distorted several subsequent judgments made by his three-year-old son. He had taken his son to visit Will Rogers's ancestral home, a dark, forbidding gothic structure. The boy did not want to go in but finally yielded to his father's urgings. As they toured the house, a tape of Will Rogers reading from one of his works was playing in the background. To passages in Rogers's narrative that had an ambiguous sound or meaning, the boy seemed to assign the darkest possible interpretations. For example, when Rogers said at one point, "Well, I tried," the boy asked his father, "Why'd he die?" Time and again, the boy's interpretations were slanted to the negative.

Given this biased filter, the development of successful personal relationships hinges powerfully on getting off to a good start. If your first experience in a relationship is positive, you engage further. But if you begin with a negative experience, things are likely to get worse.

Psychologists report that an important component of normal sympathetic responses in relationships is a subconscious impulse to mimic what your conversation partner is doing. If she smiles, you smile. If she yawns, you yawn. If she leans to one side, you lean the same way (Bavelas et al. 1986; Hatfield, Cacioppo, and Rapson 1994).

Although such mimicry turns out to be critically important, most people are not consciously aware of it. In one study, for example, psychologists had separate conversations with two groups of subjects — a control group in which the psychologists interacted without special inhibition, and a treatment group in which the psychologists consciously did not mimic the postures and other movements and expressions of their conversation partners (Chartrand and Bargh 1998). Subjects in the treatment group reported generally negative feelings toward the psychologists, while those in the control group found the same psychologists generally likeable. Apart from the suppression of physical acts of mimicry in the treatment group, no other observable details of the interactions differed between groups. This finding is consistent with the view that people may subconsciously interpret failure to mimic as signifying a deficit of sympathy.

Studies of how the appearance of married couples evolves over time also suggest that physical mimicry is an important aspect of social interaction. In one study, subjects were shown individual wedding-year photographs of a large sample of men and women, and then asked to guess which men had married which women. The accuracy of their guesses was no better than chance. But when other subjects were given the same matching task on the basis of individual photos taken after twenty-five years of marriage, the accuracy of their guesses was far better than chance (Zajonc et al. 1987). Over the course of a quarter-century of married life, apparently, the furrow of the brow, the cast of the lip, and other subtle details of facial geography seem to converge perceptibly. I have two friends, a married couple, who have been professional storytellers for several decades. As is common among storytellers, they employ exaggerated facial expressions to highlight the emotional ebbs and flows of their tales. I don't know how much they resembled one another in their youth. But people often remark on how strikingly similar they look today.

The process of bonding with another person influences, and is influenced by, physical proximity and orientation. Being too close invites a negative response, but so does being too far away, where "too close" and "too far" depend partly on cultural norms (Hall 1982). The gaze is also important (Sally 2000). Frequency and intensity of eye contact correlates strongly with the duration and intimacy of personal relationships (Patterson 1973). Among recent acquaintances, both extremely high levels of eye contact and extremely low levels often prove aversive. If experimenters seat subjects too close together, they will look at one another less frequently than if they are seated at a more comfortable distance (Argyle and Dean 1965).

The intensity of the initial interaction — even if purely the result of chance — has important consequences for long-term bonding. For example, combat troops who were under heavy shelling in the same unit corresponded with one another for many more years and much more frequently than combat troops who were not shelled heavily in the same engagement (Elder and Clipp 1988). The heavyweight fighters John Tunney and Jack Dempsey wrote to one another for years after their legendary title bouts, and did many favors for one another. They were not friends. They never even particularly liked one another, but they were thrown together in very intense circumstances that seemed to forge a bond (Heimer 1969).

Mere exposure also matters. As Robert Zajonc and his colleagues have shown, the simple fact that we have been repeatedly exposed to an initially neutral stimulus — such as a Chinese ideograph or the shape of a polygon — is enough to make us like it (Zajonc et al. 1987). Repeated exposure to persons has essentially the same effect. Relative to people we have never seen, we strongly prefer to interact with those we have seen repeatedly — in the same elevator or on the same train platform — even though we have never acknowledged one another's presence before (Brockner and Swap, 1976). As David Hume wrote, "When we have contracted a habitude and intimacy with any person; tho' in frequenting his company we have not been able to discover any very valuable quality, of which he is possess'd; yet we cannot forbear preferring him to strangers, of whose superior merit we are fully convinc'd" (Hume 1978 [1740], 352, as quoted by Sally [2000]).

Laughter also seems to be important in the development of relationships. Why do we have such a pronounced capacity to experience mirth in our interactions with one another? While other animal species may have something analogous to this capacity, even our closest relatives among primates do not have it to anything like the same degree. One possibility is that laughter not only promotes the development of social bonds, it may also be an unusually effective test of shared sympathy and understanding. People who find the same things funny often find they have many other attitudes and perceptions in common.

In short, the emergence of sympathetic bonds among people is a very complex physical, cognitive, and emotional dance. People feel one another out, respond to one another, choose to develop closer bonds with some, and abandon further contact with others.

This brief account describes only a small sample of the literature surveyed in David Sally's paper. Suffice to say, however, that this literature suggests a far more complex phenomenon than the one I sketched in *Passions Within Reason*. My simple stick-figure model gave the impression that some people feel sympathy toward others and some people do not, suggesting that the challenge is to interact selectively with those in the first group. David Sally's insight is that it would be far more descriptive to say that most people have the capacity to experience sympathy for the interests of others *under the right circumstances*. The challenge is to forge relationships in which mutual sympathy will develop sufficiently to support cooperation.

DOES SYMPATHY PREDICT COOPERATION?

Substantial evidence suggests that the same factors that promote the development of sympathetic bonds between individuals also predict an increased likelihood of cooperation. A large literature, for example, documents the importance of physical proximity and communication as predictors of the likelihood of cooperation in prisoner's dilemmas (Sally [1995] offers a review). If you are sitting next to your partner and there's a screen between you so you can't see one another, you are more likely to cooperate than if you are sitting across the table with a screen between you. You are closer, physically, in the first condition, even though you can't see one another in either case. But take the screens away and the people sitting side by side are less likely to cooperate than the people who are sitting opposite one another (Gardin et al. 1973). Apparently, the side-by-side pairs are sitting too close together to feel comfortable with extended eye contact, while those seated opposite one another do not suffer from this inhibition.

Many experiments have found that friends are much more likely to cooperate in social dilemmas with one another than are others of lesser acquaintance (Sally [2000] reviews several studies that confirm this finding). All else being constant, the longer you have known a person, the stronger your mutual bond, and the greater your assurance of cooperation. Written exchanges among participants stimulate cooperation in prisoner's dilemma experiments, but not by nearly as much as face-to-face exchanges, even if the content of the exchanges is essentially the same (Sally 1995; Valley, Moag, and Bazerman 1998).

Considered as a whole, the evidence is consistent with an affirmative answer to our question of whether moral emotions such as sympathy facilitate commitment. This evidence does not rule out alternative interpretations conclusively. But in my view, it places a substantial burden of proof on those who argue that moral emotions do not facilitate commitment.

WAS THE CAPACITY FOR SYMPATHY FORGED BY NATURAL SELECTION?

What about the second question I posed at the outset? Does available evidence provide any reason to believe that natural selection favored the evolution of sympathy at least in part *because* of its ability to solve commitment problems? A moral emotion won't be favored by natural selection merely because it motivates cooperation. It must motivate cooperation in such a way that cooperation *pays*. Does sympathy meet that test? Here, too, existing studies suggest an affirmative answer.

Consider again the two conditions that must be satisfied for a moral emotion like sympathy to facilitate mutual cooperation in one-shot prisoner's dilemmas. (By "one-shot" prisoner's dilemmas I do not mean only games that are played once between perfect strangers. Such dilemmas also include interactions among friends of long standing, as in situations in which partners are unable to discover who is responsible for the bad outcome they experience.) First, it must motivate players to cooperate, even though they would receive higher payoffs by defecting. And second, players must have statistically reliable means of predicting which potential trading partners will be trustworthy. Available evidence provides support for both conditions. In the first instance, conditions that have been shown experimentally to foster the development of sympathy have also been shown to promote cooperation in one-shot prisoner's dilemmas (see Sally [2000] for a detailed summary).

As for whether people can predict whether their partners will cooperate, some studies also show that people are aware — sometimes unconsciously, but in ways that influence observable behavior — of the degree of sympathetic bonding that exists between themselves and others. One such study, described in detail in the next chapter, suggests that experimental subjects are able to predict their partners' choices in social dilemmas on the basis of only brief periods of interaction. And as suggested by the thought experiment involving the lost envelope full of cash, substantially higher accuracy rates may be possible among people who know one another well.

How can someone tell that a potential trading partner is genuinely sympathetic to his interests? As noted earlier, psychologists have confirmed Darwin's claim that certain facial expressions are characteristic of specific emotions. Psychologists have also found that posture and other elements of body language, the pitch and timbre of the voice, the rate of respiration, and even the cadence of speech are systematically linked to underlying motivational states. Because the relevant linkages are beyond conscious control in most people, it is difficult to conceal the experience of certain emotions, and equally difficult to feign the characteristic expressions of these emotions on occasions when they are not actually experienced. For this reason, such clues provide reliable information about the emotions we trigger in others. In addition to facial expressions and other physical symptoms, we rely on reputation and a variety of other clues to predict how potential partners will treat us in specific situations (for a discussion of the role of reputation and other factors, see chapter 4 of my *Passions Within Reason*).

If we possess the capacity to discern whether others will treat our interests with respect, it is an undeniably useful one. Equally clear is that this capacity is extremely complex. As we have seen, the development of sympathetic bonds is a process involving multiple perceptual, cognitive, and emotional capacities. No one in the scientific community questions that these capacities exist in most humans. Nor does anyone question that these capacities involve specialized components of the inborn neural circuitry of humans. Nor, to my knowledge, has anyone offered a plausible theory other than natural selection that could account for the presence of such components.

Of course, the claim that moral emotions help solve commitment problems could be valid even if the relevant capacities through which those emotions act were selected for altogether different purposes — just as, for example, the human capacity to produce and enjoy music could have emerged as an accidental by-product of intellectual and emotional capabilities selected for other purposes. Indeed, theoretical considerations from the animal signaling literature suggest that moral sentiments such as sympathy almost certainly could not have *originated* purely because of their capacity to solve one-shot dilemmas.

The basic problem is that natural selection cannot be forward-looking. It cannot recognize, for example, that a series of mutations might eventually produce an individual with the capacity to solve one-shot prisoner's dilemmas, and then favor the first costly step to that end, even though it yields no immediate benefit. As I will explain presently, it is this first step that presents the difficulty, because the initial appearance of a signal would have no meaning to external observers. It would thus entail costs, but no benefits. And the Darwinian rule is that a mutation must offer an *immediate* surplus of benefits over costs, or else be consigned to the evolutionary scrap heap.

How do signals ever originate, then? Essentially by accident, according to the derivation principle developed by Niko Tinbergen (1952). The constraint imposed by this principle is clearly illustrated by the example of the dung beetle. The insect gets its name from the fact that it escapes from predators by virtue of its resemblance to a fragment of dung. Biologists argue, however, that this advantage cannot explain how this beetle came to resemble a fragment of dung in the first place. The problem is that if we start with a species whose individuals bear not the slightest resemblance to a dung fragment, a minor mutation in the direction of a dung-like appearance would not have been of any use, since, as Stephen Jay Gould asks, "can there be any edge in looking 5 percent like a turd?" (1977, 104). A mutation toward dung-like appearance will enhance fitness only if the individual's appearance *already* happened to be similar enough to a dung fragment for the mutation to have fooled the most myopic potential predator. Thus the initial path toward near-resemblance must have been essentially a matter of chance — the result of mutations that were favored for other reasons and just happened to produce a dung-like appearance in the process. Once the resemblance crosses the recognition threshold by chance, however, natural selection can be expected to fine-tune the resemblance, in the same ruthlessly effective way it fine-tunes other useful traits.

Essentially the same logic should apply to the emergence of an observable signal of a moral emotion such as sympathy. If the *only* behavioral effect of having sympathy were to motivate cooperation in one-shot prisoner's dilemmas, the first mutants with a small measure of this emotion would have enjoyed no advantage, even if their mutation happened to be accompanied by an observable signal. By virtue of its novelty, no one would have known what the signal meant, so it could not have facilitated selective interaction among sympathetic individuals. And since an undiscriminating tendency to cooperate entails costs, natural selection should have worked against sympathy, for the reasons just described.

If sympathy and other moral emotions were favored by natural selection in their earliest stages, they must therefore have conferred some other benefit. For example, perhaps a mutant with the capacity for sympathy was a more effective parent, a fitness enhancement that might have compensated for the initial costs of an indiscriminately sympathetic posture toward unrelated individuals.

A second possibility, one I explore in more depth here, is that the moral sentiments may function as self-control devices. In a world populated by utility maximizers of the sort usually assumed in economics, self-control problems would not exist. Such individuals would discount future costs and benefits at a constant exponential rate, which means that any choice that would seem best right now would also seem best in hindsight. Extensive evidence summarized by George Ainslie, however, suggests that all creatures, animal and human, tend to discount future rewards not exponentially but hyperbolically (1992). As Ainslie explains, hyperbolic discounting implies a temporary preference for "the poorer but earlier of two goals, when the earlier goal is close at hand." Seated before a bowl of salted cashews, for example, people often eat too many, and then later express sincere regret at having spoiled their dinners.

A similar time-inconsistency problem confronts people who interact in a sequence of repeated prisoner's dilemmas. In such situations, Rapoport and Chammah (1965), Axelrod (1984), and others have demonstrated the remarkable effectiveness of the tit-for-tat strategy — in which you cooperate in the first interaction, then in each successive interaction mimic whatever your partner did in the immediately preceding one. Note, however, that implementation of tit-for-tat entails an inherent self-control problem. By cooperating in the current round, the tit-for-tat player must incur a small present cost in order to receive a potentially much larger benefit in the future. In contrast, a player who defects in the current round receives a benefit immediately, whereas the costs of that action are both delayed and uncertain. Thus someone might realize he would come out ahead in the long run if he cooperated in the current interaction, yet find himself unable to resist the temptation to reap the immediate gains from defecting.

A person who is sympathetic toward potential trading partners is, by virtue of that concern, less likely than others to yield to temptation in the current interaction. Such a person would still find the gains from defecting attractive, but their allure would be mitigated by the prospect of the immediate aversive psychological reaction that would be triggered by defecting. For this reason, persons with sympathy for their trading partners would find it easier than others to implement the tit-for-tat strategy in repeated prisoner's dilemmas. To the extent that the ability to execute tit-for-tat enhances fitness, people who experienced sympathy would have fared better than those who did not, even if no observable signal of sympathy were generally recognized.

Similar reasoning applies in the case of commitment problems that entail deterrence. It will often be prudent to exact revenge against an aggressor, even at considerable personal cost, when doing so would help create a reputation that will deter future aggression. Self-interested rational persons with perfect self-control would always seek revenge whenever the future reputational gains outweighed the current costs of taking action. As before, however, the gains from a tough reputation come only in the future while the costs of vengeance-seeking come now. A person may know full well that it pays to be tough, yet still be tempted to avoid the current costs of a tough response. Thus an angry person may be more likely to behave prudently than a merely prudent person who feels no anger.

The empirical literature I described earlier documents the existence of reliable markers of sympathy and other moral emotions that influence human interaction. The animal-signaling literature provides compelling theoretical reasons for believing that both the emotions themselves and their observable signals are unlikely to have originated because of their capacity to resolve one-shot dilemmas. But given that these emotions and their markers exist, for whatever reasons, there is every reason to expect natural selection to have refined them for that purpose. We know, for example, that individual differences in emotional responsiveness are at least weakly heritable (Bruell 1970). If selective trustworthiness is advantageous and observable, natural selection should favor individual variants who are both more trustworthy and better able to communicate that fact to others.

Strategic Issues

Robert Solomon has stressed the importance of viewing emotions not as purely exogenous events but rather as something over which we often have considerable control (2003). The literature that describes how sympathetic bonds develop among people is strongly supportive of this view. In predictable ways, people react to the things we do and say to them, and we react to the things they say and do. Over time these reactions change both them and us. And because the outcomes of our choices are to a large extent predictable, decisions about the details of interpersonal interaction have a potentially strategic dimension.

Consider the decision to associate with someone. In the absence of unexpected negative feedback, and sometimes even in the presence of it, deciding to spend time with someone is tantamount to a decision to like him and to develop sympathy for his interests. If his values were initially different from yours, a decision to spend time together is likely to diminish those initial differences. Our choice of associates, therefore, is at least in part a strategic choice about the kind of values we want to hold.

The knowledge of how sympathetic bonds emerge between people also has strategic implications for the design of organizations and institutions. Most university administrations are keenly aware, for example, of how sympathy (and antipathy) can effect people's decisions in promotion cases. Accordingly, few universities delegate ultimate decision power in such cases to a faculty member's departmental colleagues. Most rely heavily on ad hoc committees composed of faculty outside the department.

Widespread prohibitions on gift-giving in institutional settings can be understood in a similar way. The fear is not, for example, that by giving a gift to a professor, the student will bribe the professor to overrule his honest judgment about the true grade she feels the student deserves. Rather, it is that the gift may foster a strong sympathetic bond between the two, which in turn may distort even the professor's most determinedly objective assessment of the student's performance.

Knowledge of the processes that forge sympathetic bonds among people also sheds light on the common practice of cronyism among corporate executives and political leaders. When such people ascend to positions of power, their first step is often to hire assistants from the ranks of their long-standing friends and subordinates. This practice invariably exposes them to the criticism that they value loyalty above competence. Yet for leaders to achieve the goals they were chosen to implement, they require subordinates who are not only competent, but also trustworthy. And because the sympathetic bonds that support trust are strongest when nurtured over a period of many years, the preference for long-term associates is, on its face, neither surprising nor blameworthy. What *would* be cause for alarm would be the observation that an executive's long-term friends and subordinates were mostly incompetent hacks. Those are choices for which we have every reason to hold a potential executive accountable.

Concluding Remarks

Traditional rational choice theories confront a painful dilemma. Without making specific assumptions about people's goals, they cannot generate testable implications for observable behavior. Most rational choice models thus assume that people pursue narrowly selfish goals. Yet people make anonymous gifts to charity, leave tips at restaurants on interstate highways, vote in presidential elections, and take a variety of other costly actions with little prospect of personal gain. Some analysts respond by introducing tastes for such behavior. But if the list of goals is not circumscribed in some way, virtually any behavior can be rationalized by simply positing a taste for it. When a man dies shortly after drinking the used crankcase oil from his car, we do not really explain anything by asserting that he must have had a powerful taste for crankcase oil.

Darwinian analysis offers a principled way of resolving this dilemma, one that is not vulnerable to the crankcase-oil objection. Evolutionary models view our goals not as ends in themselves, but as means to acquire the material resources needed for survival and reproduction. In this framework, we are free to offer a "taste for cooperation" to explain why people cooperate in one-shot prisoner's dilemmas, but only if we first can explain how having such a taste might help a person acquire the resources needed to survive and reproduce.

I have argued that cooperation in one-shot prisoner's dilemmas is sustained by bonds of sympathy among trading partners. The models I employed in my earlier work on this subject encouraged the view that some people have genuinely cooperative tendencies while others do not. I now believe it is far more descriptive to say that most people have the capacity to develop bonds of sympathy for specific trading partners under the right set of circumstances. The preference for cooperation is not an unconditional one, but rather one that depends strongly on the history of personal interaction between potential trading partners. But this amendment, in the end, is a detail. Even traditional preferences depend on context in essentially similar ways. We don't desire food at every moment, for example, but only after a suitable delay since the ingestion of our last meal.

Narrow versions of the rational choice approach leave the moral emotions completely out of the picture. Naked self-interest is not an unimportant motive, of course, and these models can help us understand much of the observed human behavioral repertoire. But there is also much that is simply beyond the reach of these models. And there is some evidence that the models themselves may do social harm by encouraging us to expect the worst from others (a point to be developed in some detail in chapter 9). By giving us a principled framework for broadening our assumptions about human motives, the Darwinian approach points the way to long-overdue enrichments of the narrow rational choice approach.

2

Can Cooperators Find One Another?

As DISCUSSED in the preceding chapter, cooperation in one-shot social dilemmas can be a rewarding strategy, but only under certain conditions. The essential requirement is that cooperating individuals somehow manage to pair off with others who also cooperate. Can we reliably sort ourselves in this way? This chapter reports the results of a study in which my Cornell colleagues Tom Gilovich and Dennis Regan and I attempted to answer this question experimentally.

THE BASIC EXPERIMENT

Our experiment involved volunteer subjects who played a one-shot prisoner's dilemma game with one another. Many were Cornell undergraduates recruited from courses in which the prisoner's dilemma was an item on the syllabus. Others were given a detailed preliminary briefing about the game. At the end of the experiment each subject was required to answer several questions to verify that he or she had indeed understood the consequences of different combinations of choices in the game. (Virtually every subject answered these questions correctly.)

Subjects met in groups of three and each was told that he or she would play the game once with each of the other two subjects. The payoff matrix, shown in figure 2.1, was the same for each play of the game. Subjects were told that the games would be played once only with each partner, for real money, and that none of the players would learn how their partners had responded in each play of the game. (More below on how confidentiality was maintained.)

In figure 2.1 note that when each player cooperates, each gets a payoff of $2, for a total payoff of $4, the highest total among the four cells in the table. Note also, however, that each player's dominant strategy is to

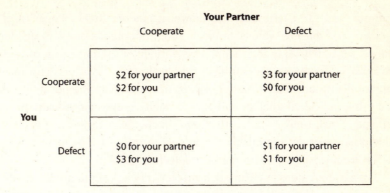

Figure 2.1 Payoffs for the Prisoner's Dilemma Experiment

defect. If your partner cooperates, for example, you get $3 by defecting instead of the $2 you would have gotten by cooperating; and if your partner defects, you get $1 by defecting instead of the $0 you would have gotten by cooperating. Thus, as in all prisoner's dilemmas, the collectively optimal strategy for the payoff matrix in figure 2.1 is mutual cooperation, but the individually optimal strategy is defection.

Before playing the game, each group of three subjects met for a period that varied from ten to thirty minutes. The purpose of this meeting was to allow subjects to get acquainted and glean whatever information they could that might be relevant for predicting cooperation. Following this meeting, each subject was taken to a separate room and asked to fill out a form indicating his response (cooperate or defect) to each of the other two players. In addition, subjects were asked to predict how each of their partners would respond. They were also asked to record a number from fifty to one hundred indicating how confident they felt about each of these predictions. A response of fifty meant that the prediction was no better than chance, one of one hundred that they were completely confident of it. Intermediate numbers indicated intermediate degrees of confidence.

After the subjects had filled out their forms, the results were tallied and the payments disbursed. Each subject received a single payment that was the sum of three separate amounts: (1) the payoff from the game with the first partner; (2) the payoff from the game with the second partner; and (3) a term that was drawn at random from a large list of positive and negative values. Subjects could not observe these three elements separately, only their sum. The purpose of the random term was to make it impossible for a subject to infer from his total payment how any of the other subjects had played. It prevented both the possibility of inferring individual choices and also of inferring even group patterns of choice. Thus, unlike most earlier experiments with one-shot prisoner's dilemmas, ours did not enable the subject to infer what happened even when each (or none) of his partners defected.

We also took steps to ensure that subjects' choices could not be identified by the experimenter. To achieve this result, we employed two experimenters, a principal and an assistant. The principal was the one who guided subjects through the experiment, and was the only one with whom subjects had significant contact. He instructed them to put a code word on their questionnaires, explaining that, when they finished, his assistant, who would have only fleeting contact with them, would collect their questionnaires and shuffle them before computing how much each subject should be paid. Once the proper payment for each subject was computed, the assistant would report to the principal how much each code name should receive. The assistant then left the lab. Subjects were told that this procedure, in combination with the random term, would prevent the principal experimenter from knowing how any individual subject had responded.

To explore the role of communication, participants were assigned to one of three conditions, each permitting a different level of pre-game interaction. In the "unlimited" group, subjects were given thirty minutes to meet with one another and were told that they could discuss their strategies for playing the game and, if they wished, make promises to cooperate. They were also told, however, that the anonymity of their responses would render such promises unenforceable. With the permission of subjects in several of the unlimited groups, we taped their conversations, during which they invariably made promises to cooperate. (Why would anyone say, "I'm going to defect."?) The "intermediate" group was given instructions identical to the unlimited group's except that intermediate subjects were told they could not make promises regarding play. Finally, subjects in the "limited" group were not permitted

TABLE 2.1
Three Experimental Conditions

Experimental Condition	Pre-game meeting period	Permitted communication	Number of subjects
Unlimited	30 minutes	Complete freedom of communication, including freedom to make promises to cooperate	99
Intermediate	Up to 30 minutes	Promises not permitted; otherwise, complete freedom	84
Limited	Up to 10 minutes	Communication about the game not permitted; otherwise, complete freedom	84

to discuss the prisoner's dilemma at all and were given no more than ten minutes to get acquainted. These experimental conditions and the number of subjects assigned to each are summarized in table 2.1.

RESULTS

Consistent with the findings of numerous other experimental studies, we found that the overall rate of cooperation rose when subjects were given more opportunity to communicate (for surveys of these studies, see Dawes [1980] and Sally [1995]). As shown in figure 2.2, the cooperation rate was 45.2 percent for the limited group, 48.8 percent for the intermediate group, and 73.7 percent for the unlimited group. In each of the three groups, subjects overestimated the overall frequency of cooperation. The predicted cooperation rate for the unlimited groups was 81.3 percent, while both the intermediate and limited groups predicted 62.5 percent.

Despite the fact that our random payoff term assured confidentiality, well more than half (57 percent) of our subjects did not play the dominant strategy of defection. The cooperation rates we found lie in the range of results found in previous studies. In view of the added step we took to assure anonymity, our findings provide even stronger evidence of the inadequacy of the narrow self-interest model.

Because our general concern here is to discover whether cooperation in one-shot dilemmas can be an economically rewarding strategy, the

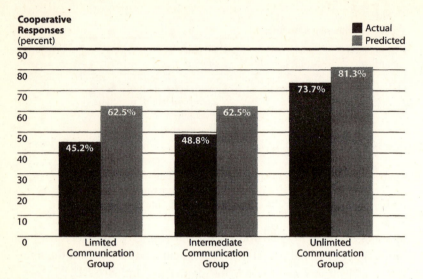

Figure 2.2 Percentage of Cooperative Responses

data of greatest interest are those pertaining to the accuracy of the predictions concerning specific players. We will consider the performance
of the different groups in turn.

Of the 161 partners who were predicted to play cooperatively in the
unlimited communication group, 130, or 80.7 percent, actually did so.
(See figure 2.3.) Of the 37 people predicted to defect, 21, or 56.8 percent, actually did so. How accurate are these predictions? For the unlimited communications group, a reasonable benchmark is the expected
accuracy of a subject who randomly predicts cooperation 81.3 percent of
the time and defection 18.7 percent of the time (the rates with which
subjects predicted cooperation and defection, respectively). Since the actual rates of cooperation and defection were 73.7 percent and 26.3 percent, respectively, the overall average accuracy rate for such a subject
would be

$$(.813)(73.7) + (.187)(26.3) = 64.8 \text{ percent,}$$

or 11.5 percentage points lower than the 76.3 percent accuracy rate
achieved by the unlimited communications group. On the assumption
that subjects' beliefs about the likelihood of defection are accurately

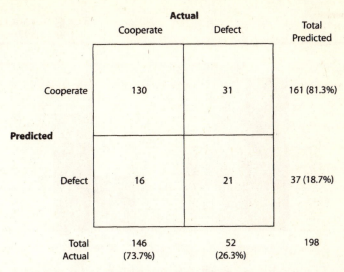

Figure 2.3 Predicted vs. Actual Behavior: Unlimited Communication Group

measured by the overall rate of predicted defection, the likelihood of such a high overall accuracy rate occurring by chance is less than one in one thousand.[1] Henceforth, all comparisons between actual and chance accuracy rates are reported in terms of this revealed-beliefs benchmark.

Breaking out the performance of unlimited communication subjects by type of prediction (see figure 2.4), we see that a random prediction of cooperation would have been accurate 73.7 percent of the time as compared with an actual accuracy rate of 80.7 percent. This 7-percent increment over chance performance may not seem large in proportional terms, but bear in mind that improvements over chance performance become increasingly difficult to achieve as the base rate for a category increases well past 50 percent. (In the limiting case, when the base rate for a category approaches 100 percent, it becomes almost impossible to predict better than chance.) The contrast between the accuracy of actual and chance predictions is much more dramatic for predictions of defection, for here the category base rate is well below 50 percent and subjects' predictions overall run strongly counter to the base rate. For the unlimited group, predictions of defection were accurate 56.8 percent of the time, more than twice the 26.3 percent accuracy rate of a random prediction.

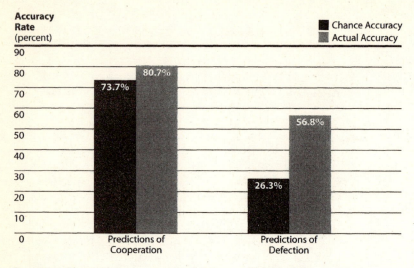

Figure 2.4 Chance Accuracy vs. Actual Accuracy: Unlimited Communication
Group

For the unlimited communication group, patterns in the confidence
figures that subjects recorded for their predictions were also supportive of
the hypothesis that people can achieve mutual cooperation in one-shot
social dilemmas. These figures, recall, are the numbers between fifty and
one hundred that indicate the level of confidence the subject feels in
each prediction. Subjects were usually more confident in their estimates
than subsequent experience warranted (see, for example, Lichtenstein,
Fischoff, and Phillips [1982], who argue that overconfidence is a general
human tendency). Even so, the patterns we found were broadly consistent with the view that people have some sense, even on the basis of
brief personal interaction, of when their predictions are most likely to be
accurate. In keeping with their implicit estimate of the base rate of cooperation, subjects in the unlimited group were more confident of their
predictions of cooperation (average confidence level = 85.66) than of
their predictions of defection (76.46). More important, they placed
greater confidence in the predictions of both types that subsequently
proved correct (86.82 for cooperation, 78.76 for defection) than in those
that proved incorrect (80.78 for cooperation, 73.44 for defection). As
shown in figure 2.5, of the 160 predictions made with a confidence level

**Accuracy
Rate**
(percent)

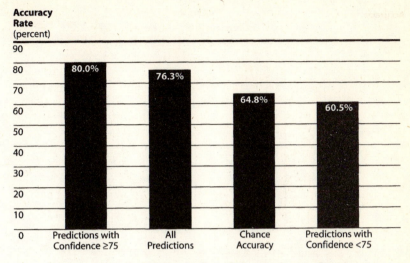

Figure 2.5 Accuracy vs. Confidence: Unlimited Communication Group

of 75 or higher by subjects in the unlimited communication group, 80 percent were correct, as compared with only 60.5 percent of the 38 predictions made with a confidence level below 75.

The intermediate and limited subjects did not predict as proficiently as did those in the unlimited group. The relevant data on the accuracy of individual predictions of subjects in these groups are displayed in figures 2.6 and 2.7.

If we again take subjects' rates of predicted cooperation and defection as reflecting their beliefs about the respective likelihoods of these behaviors, the expected rate of correct predictions for a subject in the intermediate group who randomly predicts cooperation 62.5 percent of the time is given by

$$(.625)(48.8) + (.375)(51.2) = 49.7 \text{ percent,}$$

which is virtually the same as the actual rate of correct prediction for this group, 49.4 percent. The corresponding benchmark of correct predictions for the limited group is

$$(.625)(45.2) + (.375)(54.8) = 48.8 \text{ percent,}$$

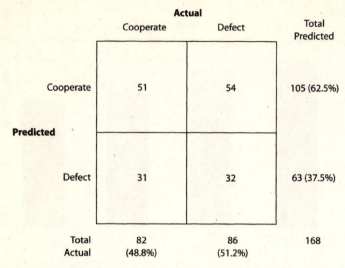

Figure 2.6 Predicted vs. Actual Responses: Intermediate Communications

Actual

	Cooperate	Defect	Total Predicted
Predicted Cooperate	51	54	105 (62.5%)
Defect	31	32	63 (37.5%)
Total Actual	82 (48.8%)	86 (51.2%)	168

Actual

	Cooperate	Defect	Total Predicted
Predicted Cooperate	50	55	105 (62.5%)
Defect	26	37	63 (37.5%)
Total Actual	76 (45.2%)	92 (54.8%)	168

Figure 2.7 Predicted vs. Actual Responses: Limited Communications

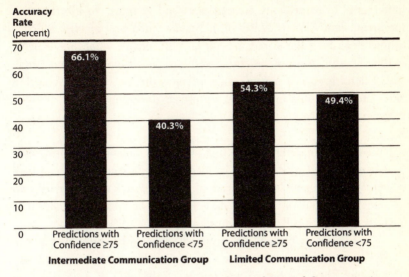

Figure 2.8 Accuracy vs. Confidence: Intermediate and Limited Communications Groups

which is also little different from the group's actual rate of 51.8 percent correct predictions.

As was the case for the unlimited group, however, subjects in the other two groups were more accurate when they expressed relatively high confidence in their predictions. (See figure 2.8.) This was especially true for subjects in the intermediate group, who predicted with 66.1 percent accuracy when their confidence levels were 75 or higher, as compared with only 40.3 percent accuracy when their confidence levels were below 75. The corresponding figures for the limited group were 54.3 percent and 49.4 percent.

STRANGERS VS. CLOSE ACQUAINTANCES

Unlike real-world experience, our experiments do not let us see how people behave under varied and stressful circumstances. Moreover, even if they did, there would remain the difficulty of interpreting individual differences in expressions, mannerisms, and gestures. To illustrate this problem, Paul Ekman quotes Tom Brokaw, then host of NBC's Today Show, describing the signals he found most reliable when interviewing public figures: "Most of the clues I get from people are verbal, not physical. I don't look at a person's face for signs that he is lying. What I'm after are convoluted answers or sophisticated evasions" (1985, 90–91). Ekman goes on to say:

> A few studies of deceit support Brokaw's hunch, finding that some people when they lied were indirect in their reply, circumlocutious, and gave more information than was requested. Other research studies have shown just the opposite: most people are too smart to be evasive and indirect in their replies. Tom Brokaw might miss those liars. A worse hazard would be to misjudge a truthful person who happens to be convoluted or evasive in his speech. A few people always speak this way. For them it is not a sign of lying; it is just the way they talk. (1985, 91)

In short, what is a reliable clue to deceit in one person may simply be a normal feature of some other person's repertoire. To read behavioral clues accurately, we must first know baseline behavior, and this will often take much more than a brief meeting.

To see whether length of acquaintanceship matters, we compared the performance of strangers with that of undergraduate sophomores, juniors, and seniors who belong to the same fraternity or sorority. To forestall possible confusion, we should state clearly here that even though the fraternity and sorority subjects can expect to interact extensively with one another in the future, our experiment still confronts them with a one-shot prisoner's dilemma. As with the other subjects, defecting will produce the highest payoff in material terms and will not damage their reputations in any way. The results for this version of the experiment are summarized in figure 2.9.

As expected, the cooperation rate observed among close acquaintances in figure 2.9 (94.44 percent) is dramatically higher than for the sample as a whole (70.64 percent). From a total of fifty-four predictions, there were only three predictions of defection, and one of these three

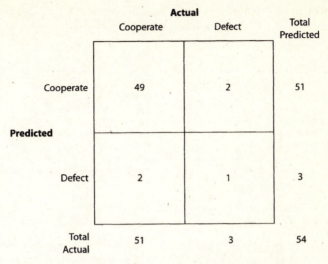

Figure 2.9 Predicted vs. Actual Responses: Fraternity/Sorority Group

was accurate. With so little variation in the rate of predicted cooperation, however, we cannot state with confidence that close acquaintances are better than strangers at spotting defectors in their midst.

MALES VS. FEMALES

Most of our three-person experimental groups consisted of persons of the same sex, and we observed significantly different patterns of behavior for males and females. In the unlimited interaction version of the experiment, for example, males had a cooperation rate of only 66.4 percent, as compared with 78.2 percent for females. As the responses summarized in figures 2.10 and 2.11 indicate, the accuracy of predictions was considerably greater for females than for males. When a female subject predicted defection, for example, she was right 60 percent of the time. In contrast, males who predicted defection were correct only 44.7 percent of the time. The difference in these accuracy rates actually understates the female advantage, because the base rate of defection was so much lower among females (21.8 percent) than among males (33.6 percent).

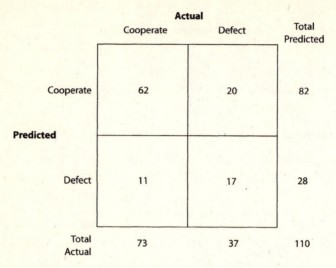

Figure 2.10 Predicted vs. Actual Responses for Males in the Unlimited Version

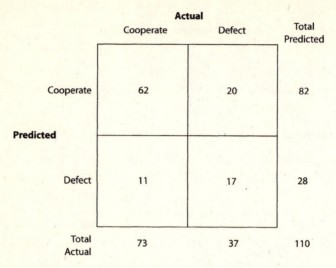

Figure 2.11 Predicted vs. Actual Responses for Females in the Unlimited Version

RELATIONSHIP TO PREVIOUS FINDINGS

Our search of the voluminous literature on the prisoner's dilemma turned up only one previous study that addressed whether subjects could predict the behavior of their partners. The design of that study, by Dawes, McTavish, and Shaklee (1977), differed from ours in several important respects. For instance, theirs involved an eight-person commons dilemma as compared to our two-person prisoner's dilemma. Also, while they, too, ran several conditions that differed in the amount of pre-game interaction permitted, none of their conditions afforded more than ten minutes of communication. Especially in comparison with our unlimited communication group, the larger groups and shorter meeting times of their study combine to yield significantly reduced opportunities for interactions between subjects.

Perhaps for this reason, the subjects studied by Dawes, McTavish, and Shaklee did not predict individual cooperation and defection with nearly the accuracy of our unlimited communication subjects. Pooling their results across four communication conditions in one version of their experiment, Dawes, McTavish, and Shaklee report that subjects' predictive accuracy was only three percentage points better than chance — in their words, a "tiny" margin (1977, 6). They go on to report that in a second version, subjects' predictive accuracy was actually 2 percent below chance.

Now, the main purpose of the Dawes, McTavish, and Shaklee study was not to measure predictive accuracy per se, but to assess how a player's own behavior was related to the behavior he or she predicted in others. Perhaps for this reason, the authors did not report their findings on predictive accuracy in detail. In particular, they did not break down their actual-vs.-chance accuracy calculations for the four different communication conditions in their experiment. Using information reported in their paper, however, we were able to reconstruct these values. Of special interest is the result for their maximum communication group, which, like our unlimited group, permitted subjects to make verbal promises to cooperate. For this group, the actual base rate of cooperation was 73 percent, as compared with a predicted rate of 90 percent. Chance accuracy levels for this group are thus given by

$$(.90)(73.0) + (.10)(27.0) = 68.4 \text{ percent},$$

which is more than 7 percent lower than the 75.6 percent actual accuracy rate for their maximum communication group. Although this is smaller than the 11.5-percent margin observed for our unlimited group, it is nonetheless a significant increment over chance prediction. The difference between their margin and ours may be plausibly attributed to the more extensive communication opportunities provided in our experiment.

DISCUSSION

Both our findings and those of Dawes, McTavish, and Shaklee are broadly consistent with the hypothesis that, under at least some circumstances, people can make better-than-chance predictions about how their partners will play in one-shot prisoner's dilemmas. We are quick to emphasize, however, that these findings do not imply the existence of stable personality types called cooperators and defectors. On the contrary, 22 percent of our subjects did not consistently follow either strategy, cooperating with one of their partners but defecting on the other.[2] The remaining subjects followed the same strategy in both of their games. In both games, 46 percent cooperated while 32 percent defected. But this obviously does not imply that they would do likewise in every situation. Indeed, the observed differences in cooperation rates across our three communication conditions make it clear that the tendency to cooperate depends very strongly on how the interactions between subjects are structured.

A pattern observed in all experimental conditions, but much more pronounced in the unlimited group, was for subjects to behave the same way they predicted their partners would (Dawes, McTavish, and Shaklee [1977] report a similar finding). In the unlimited group, for example, 88 percent of the subjects who predicted their partners would cooperate also cooperated themselves. Similarly, 86 percent of the subjects who predicted defection also defected themselves.

In a debriefing session in this experiment, we asked subjects to fill out a form explaining why they predicted cooperation from some partners, defection from others. Their responses were generally consistent with the notion that cooperation may be explained less by individual traits of character (the naïve characterization of my stick-figure model described in chapter 1) than by the nature of the interactions between specific partners. For example, subjects would offer reasons like "we had a pleasant conversation" when explaining their prediction that a specific partner would cooperate, or like "we really didn't seem to hit it off" when explaining why they thought another partner would defect.

Concluding Remarks

For cooperation in one-shot social dilemmas to be a rewarding strategy in material terms, cooperating individuals somehow manage to pair off with others who also cooperate. The experiments reported in this chapter are consistent with the hypothesis that many people do in fact have the capacity to interact selectively in this way. Moreover, our experiments with our unlimited communications group suggest that the accuracy rates needed to support mutually beneficial cooperation can be achieved even on the basis of relatively brief interaction, at least when the stakes are small. A subject in that group who was predicted to defect was more than twice as likely to do so than the 26.3 percent overall sample base rate for defection. It appears plausible to conjecture that even higher predictive accuracy should be possible for people who have known one another for extended periods of time. Thus, it does not seem fanciful to suppose that cooperators can find one another, at least in a statistical sense. That ability can sustain a stable equilibrium in which people who cooperate in one-shot social dilemmas achieve payoffs that match those of people who defect.

Notes

1. Treating each prediction as an independent observation, the relevant chi-square statistic from figure 2.6 is 21.83 ($p < .001$). Allowing for the possibility that the two predictions made by each subject are not independent, the overall

accuracy rates are still significant: The relevant chi-square statistics for the tables of subjects' first and second predictions are 6.10 ($p < .02$) and 18.91 ($p < .001$), respectively.

2. This feature could not be observed in the Dawes, McTavish, and Shaklee experiments, where each subject made only one choice.

3

Adaptive Rationality and the Moral Emotions

ALTHOUGH THEY HAVE BEEN the subject of intense discussion for literally thousands of years, the terms rationality and morality remain shrouded in ambiguity. Our discussion in chapter 1 helps to identify some of the sources of this ambiguity and suggests a conceptual framework that can help to reduce it somewhat, by taking account of the strategic role of moral emotions in social interaction. This same framework, however, suggests that ambiguity cannot be fully purged from the concepts of rationality and morality.

There are many conceptions of rationality, each with its own strengths and weaknesses. Much of the ambiguity concerning rationality stems from the simple fact that no single conception has managed to prevail over its competitors. I illustrate by considering two specific conceptions, the present-aim standard and the self-interest standard.

The present-aim standard holds that a person is rational if she is efficient in the pursuit of whatever objectives she happens to hold at the moment of action. This standard makes no attempt to evaluate the objectives themselves. Its appealing feature is that it enables us to accommodate the plurality of goals that most people actually hold.

But this virtue turns out also to be a handicap, for it keeps the present-aim model from making many testable predictions about behavior. Recall the example cited in chapter 1 in which someone drinks a gallon of used crankcase oil from his car, then writhes in agony and dies. This example poses no problem for the present-aim theorist, who is free to assert that the man must have really *liked* crankcase oil.

The self-interest conception of rationality avoids this problem by committing itself to a specific assumption about preferences: it holds that a person is rational if he is efficient in the pursuit of self-interested objectives. Of course, the modifier "self-interested" is itself ambiguous. Some writers interpret it to mean only the acquisition of material wealth; others interpret it more broadly, embracing not just wealth, but also aesthetic pleasures and various, other less materialistic concerns. But in all cases, the self-interest model excludes concerns about honor, duty, the welfare of the poor, and other manifestly "unselfish" motives.

Quite apart from the fact that self-interest is an important human motive, a clear attraction of the self-interest model is that it facilitates testable predictions about behavior. Given the opportunities a self-interested person faces in any given situation, the model predicts what he or she will do. Moreover, the model's predictions are often remarkably accurate. Its proponents have demonstrated its capacity to explain behavior across an impressive spectrum of domains.

The self-interest model's shortcoming is that a great deal of human behavior appears flatly inconsistent with it. People donate blood, they return unwanted pesticides to governmental disposal facilities rather than simply pour them down their basement drains, they help strangers in distress, and in countless other ways they appear to subordinate narrow self-interest to the pursuit of other goals. The self-interest model is simple and elegant. Unfortunately, it is also often wrong.

With the obvious deficiencies and strengths of each standard of rationality in view, it is hardly a puzzle that multiple, conflicting standards continue to be widely used. This would be confusing enough even if authors were always clear about which standard they had in mind. In practice, however, the problem is compounded by the fact that authors rarely acknowledge that there are competing standards of rationality.

There are perhaps even more conceptions of morality than of rationality, but for the purposes of this discussion I will focus on a feature that is common in many conceptions, namely, the subordination of one's own narrow interests to the interests of a broader community. The narrow self-interest standard of rationality is incompatible with morality thus conceived. The present-aim standard, by contrast, allows this conception of morality, but only in the case in which someone happens to have a taste for behaving morally. For someone who lacks that taste, the present-aim model joins the self-interest model in denying the compatibility of rationality and morality.

No matter how rationality and morality are defined, both concepts have considerable motivational force. Most people seem to want to think of themselves as moral and also to think of themselves as rational. When a person's behavior is characterized by others as immoral or irrational, she usually responds in one of two ways: by changing her behavior, or by changing her beliefs about rationality and morality. Instances of moral behaviors being adopted to win approval from others are familiar. Less common are cases in which people choose immoral behaviors to bolster their sense of rationality, but I will discuss evidence of such responses in chapter 9.

The second response — changing beliefs to accommodate behavior — is called "dissonance reduction" by psychologists, and it, too, is common. People who focus on advancing their own narrow interests tend to be drawn to beliefs about morality that stress the social gains that often spring from self-interested behavior. Others whose behavior is more attuned to community interests are more likely to hold moral beliefs that emphasize the need for self-restraint.

With these brief remarks, I have tried to illustrate why confusion and ambiguity might be inherent properties of the concepts of rationality and morality. In the next section, I will propose a third standard of rationality, which I call "adaptive rationality," that promises to narrow the scope of this ambiguity. Adaptive rationality incorporates the most attractive features of both the self-interest and present-aim standards of rationality and at the same time sheds some of the worst deficiencies of each. In the process, it also helps to limit some of the conflicts between morality and other conceptions of rationality. But it also makes clear that some conflicts are unavoidable.

ADAPTIVE RATIONALITY

Rationality — in both the self-interest and present-aim conceptions — involves the choice of efficient means to achieve given ends. Adaptive rationality retains the requirement that people be efficient in their choice of means. But unlike the other conceptions, which take goals as given, adaptive rationality regards goals themselves as objects of choice and, as such, subject to a similar efficiency requirement.

Now, the idea of subjecting an individual's goals to an efficiency test may strike many readers as odd. Ever since Bentham, who insisted that a taste for poetry was no better than a taste for pushpins, the rational choice tradition has emphasized that individual preferences are beyond scrutiny. By what standard could we possibly evaluate an individual's choice of goals?

One way to approach this question is the one adopted in chapter 1, in which preferences were analyzed in an evolutionary context. Darwin's theory of natural selection, enriched to allow for the influence of cultural and other environmental forces during development, is the only theory that provides a coherent account of how the components of human motivation were forged. In this framework, the design criterion for a preference is the same as for an arm or a leg or an eye: To what extent does it assist the individual in the struggle to acquire the resources required for survival and reproduction? If it works better than the available alternatives, selection pressure will favor it. Otherwise, selection pressure will work against it.

At first glance, this theoretical structure might seem to throw its weight squarely behind the self-interest conception of rationality. Indeed, if natural selection favors the traits and behaviors that maximize individual reproductive fitness, and if we *define* behaviors that enhance personal fitness as selfish, then self-interest becomes the only viable human motive by definition. This tautology was a central message of much of the sociobiological literature of the 1970s and 1980s.

As we saw in chapter 1, however, the issues are not so simple, for there are many situations in which individuals whose only goal is self-interest are likely to be especially bad at acquiring and holding resources. We saw, for example, that people motivated by moral emotions such as sympathy can reap the fruits of mutual cooperation in social dilemmas if they are able to identify and interact selectively with others who are similarly motivated. And in chapter 2 we saw that people do appear to have the capacity to achieve such selective interaction, even on the basis of only brief periods of conversation.

Knowing this, even a rational, self-interested individual would have every reason to choose preferences that were not narrowly self-interested. Of course, people do not choose their preferences in any literal sense. The point is that if moral sentiments can be reliably discerned by others, then the complex interaction of genes and culture can sustain prefer-ences that lead people to subordinate narrow self-interest in the pursuit of other goals.

AN EQUILIBRIUM MIX OF MOTIVES

It might seem that if moral sentiments help solve important commit-ment problems, then evolutionary forces would assure that everyone have a full measure of these sentiments. But a closer look at the inter-play between selfish and altruistic motives suggests that this is unlikely to be the case. As in chapter 1, consider an environment populated by two types of people, cooperators and defectors. These people earn their liveli-hood by interacting in pairs, and the commitment problem they con-front is the one-shot prisoner's dilemma.

As we saw earlier, if cooperators and defectors were perfectly indis-tinguishable, interactions would occur on a random basis and the aver-age payoffs would always be larger for the defectors (again, owing to the dominance of defection in all prisoner's dilemmas). In evolutionary models, the rule governing population dynamics is that each type repro-duces in proportion to its material payoff relative to other types. This implies that if the two types were indistinguishable, the eventual result would be extinction for the cooperators. In highly simplified form, this is the Darwinian story that inclines many social scientists to believe that self-interest is the only important human motive.

But we also saw that if cooperators were distinguishable at a glance from defectors, then interaction would no longer take place on a ran-dom basis. Rather, the cooperators would pair off systematically with one another to reap the benefits of mutual cooperation. Defectors would be left to interact with one another and would receive the lower payoff associated with these pairings. The eventual result in that case was that the defectors would be driven to extinction.

Neither of these two polar cases seems descriptive of actual popula-tions, which typically contain a mix of cooperators and defectors. Such a mixed population is precisely the result we get if we make one small modification to the original story. Again suppose that cooperators are observably different from defectors but that some effort is required to make the distinction. If the population initially consisted almost entirely of cooperators, it would not pay to expend this effort because one would be overwhelmingly likely to achieve a high payoff merely by interacting at random with another person. In such an environment, cooperators would cease to be vigilant in their choice of trading partners. Defectors would then find a ready pool of victims, and their resulting higher payoffs would cause their share of the total population to grow.

As defectors became more numerous, however, it would begin to pay cooperators to exercise greater vigilance. With sufficiently many defectors in the population, cooperators would be vigilant in the extreme, and we would again see pairings among like types only. That, in turn, would cause the prevalence of cooperators to grow. At some point, a stable balance would be struck in which cooperators were just vigilant enough to prevent further encroachment by defectors. The average payoff to the two types would be the same, and their population shares would remain constant. There would be, in other words, a stable environmental niche for each type.

Ecological models like the one sketched here can also be offered in support of a more nuanced portrait of individual human motivation. For example, rather than starting with a population in which people are exclusively one type or the other, we might begin with individuals with some mix of different motives. Such models would lead us to expect an equilibrium in which each individual experiences both selfish and altruistic motives to varying degrees.

But although the details of the story may differ according to the particular model chosen, ecological models as a group have an important feature in common: Each stresses that we should not expect a world populated exclusively by the *homo economicus* caricature that populates conventional rational choice models. Such creatures may survive at the margins in environments in which monitoring costs make it too expensive to ferret them out. But they hardly represent a sensible basis on which to ground a universal science of human behavior.

The adaptive rationality framework provides theoretical underpinning for a remarkably commonsensical portrait of human nature. It tells us that people are driven by a combination of selfish and altruistic motives, just as experience seems to suggest. The mix of motives is highly variable across individuals, yet polar cases are by no means common.

The adaptive rationality approach also retains the most important strengths of both the present-aim and self-interest conceptions of rationality while eliminating the most glaring weaknesses of each. For example, like the present-aim standard, it permits the incorporation of a broad repertoire of human objectives. But unlike the present-aim standard, it does not give investigators a free hand to assume any objective that might prove convenient in a given context. Under the adaptive rationality standard, a goal can be included only if a plausible case can be made that persons who hold that goal are not handicapped in their efforts to acquire and hold resources. Like the self-interest standard, the adaptive rationality standard makes a commitment to a given repertoire of tastes and is thus equally able to generate refutable hypotheses about behavior. But because the repertoire of tastes it includes is broader than that of the self-interest model, the adaptive rationality model can accommodate a much larger suite of behaviors than can the self-interest model.

Another advantage of the adaptive rationality model is that it narrows the range of inconsistency between rationality and morality. By accommodating preferences for moral behavior, it is like the present-aim standard in saying that morality and rationality are often consistent. At the same time, it preserves the possibility of a distinction between the two concepts. Not everyone need have moral preferences under the adaptive rationality standard, and, indeed, if people's preferences are costly to discern, there will almost certainly be at least some individuals whose preferences are not moral. The real departure of the adaptive rationality standard on this dimension is from the self-interest standard, which holds that rationality and morality are never compatible.

LINKS TO OTHER WORK

The adaptive rationality model is an evolutionary game-theoretic model of the kind described by Brian Skyrms (1998). Also in keeping with the class of models that Skyrms discusses, it is a model in which cooperation evolves through correlated pairings. The key to the evolution of cooperation in these models is that cooperators interact with one another with a frequency higher than their share of the total population. Without this property, defection remains the only evolutionarily stable strategy.

There are numerous other antecedents and close relatives of the adaptive rationality model in the literature. The concept of commitment problems traces to Thomas Schelling's 1960 book, *The Strategy of Conflict*. Schelling (1978) went on to suggest that emotions might help solve commitment problems. George Akerlof published an elaboration of this idea in 1983. Amartya Sen acknowledged the benefits of non-self-interested behavior in a 1985 paper, and that same year David Gauthier's book, *Morals By Agreement*, described how behavioral predispositions might solve various commitment problems. Edward McClennen's work on resolute choice (1990) builds on a very similar idea. Jack Hirshleifer also explores these issues in a 1987 paper, "On the Emotions as Guarantors of Threats and Promises." I investigate the equilibrium properties of the model under imperfect signaling in a 1987 paper, and Alan Gibbard discusses similar themes in a 1990 book.

All of these works assume that the relevant behavioral predispositions can somehow be made known to outsiders, if only with some uncertainty. My 1988 book, *Passions Within Reason*, focuses on the problem of mimicry and tries to spell out how information about behavioral predispositions can be credibly transmitted in environments in which individuals have strong incentives to misrepresent themselves.

Adaptive Rationality and Voodoo Causation

The adaptive rationality model also sheds light on the problem of "voodoo causation" that arises in models with correlated pairings. Skyrms (1998) describes this problem, although not by that name. Max and Moritz must play a one-shot prisoner's dilemma with one another, and each believes, correctly, that their probabilities of choosing the same strategy are highly correlated. Should knowledge of this correlation change the attractiveness, in purely material terms, of cooperating? Under conventional expected utility models, the answer is no, for the correlations do not change the fact that defection is a dominant strategy. Even though their modes of play are correlated, neither player's play has any causal influence on the other's. Choosing to cooperate in the belief that this will make one's partner more likely to cooperate is thus to believe in "voodoo causation."

Yet something strikingly akin to voodoo causation emerges from a more complete account of the dynamics of interaction under adaptive rationality. When behavioral predispositions cannot be observed with certainty, cooperative individuals must decide whether to interact with a given partner on the basis of an estimate of the probability that that partner will also cooperate. These estimates will depend on information specific to the individual partner, and also on the perceived base rate of cooperators in the population of interacting individuals. A cooperator will thus be more likely to interact with a given partner when that base rate is high than when it is low.

Now suppose that a defector experiences an epiphany and decides to become a cooperator. By so doing, he increases the base rate of cooperators in the interacting population. This, in turn, raises all other cooperators' estimates of the likelihood that a given potential partner is a cooperator. Some cooperators whose initial pessimistic estimates kept them on the sidelines will now be moved to join the interacting population, raising the base rate of cooperators in that population still further. When and if a new equilibrium is reached, it will be one in which there is a larger — possibly substantially larger — share of cooperators in the interacting population.

Through its effect on others' estimates of the likelihood of cooperation, then, an individual's decision to cooperate in a one-shot prisoner's dilemma may indeed cause others also to cooperate. Of course, there will be no causal effect on his own partner in his first venture, so in this sense the traditional model's position on voodoo causation is sustained. Yet a person's initial decision to cooperate may nonetheless be said to have caused an increase in cooperation in subsequent encounters.

Do Conceptions of Rationality and Morality Matter?

Are conceptions of rationality and morality of concern only to social scientists, philosophers, and other academics, or do they have implications for behavior in the broader community? Given the apparent motivational force of these concepts, the different conceptions may indeed give rise to different behavior.

Views about human nature have important practical consequences. In the public policy arena, they affect the conduct of foreign affairs, the design and scope of economic regulation, and the structure of taxation. In the world of commerce, they dictate corporate strategies for preventing workers from shirking, for bargaining with unions, and for setting prices. In our personal lives, they affect how we choose mates and jobs, even how we spend our incomes.

More important, our beliefs about human nature help shape human nature itself. Our ideas about the limits of human potential mold what we aspire to become. They also shape what we teach our children, both at home and in the schools.

The adaptive rationality model and self-interest model paint strikingly different pictures not only of human nature, but also of its consequences for material welfare. The traditional self-interest model says that people who love, who feel guilty when they cheat, vengeful when they are wronged, or envious when they get less than their fair share will often behave in ways that reduce their material payoffs. But the adaptive rationality model tells us that precisely because of this, they may also enjoy opportunities that would not be available to a purely opportunistic person. In many cases, a person or society armed with this knowledge will make better choices than one exposed only to the self-interest tradition.

ADAPTIVE RATIONALITY AND CONSEQUENTIALIST MORAL REASONING

Emerging medical technologies have confronted both patients and practitioners with a host of challenging new ethical questions. Consider, for example, a family with a daughter who is dying of leukemia and whose only hope is for a bone-marrow transplant from a closely matched donor. With time running out in the search for a suitable donor, is it morally acceptable for the girl's parents to conceive a child with the explicit intention of harvesting her bone marrow to help save the life of her older sister? Traditional religious or other deontological moral theories, which rest on a core of basic moral principles that are held to be self-evidently true, often provide little useful guidance. The Ten Commandments, for example, do not speak to this particular question.

This problem has led to renewed interest in consequentialist moral theories, which hold that the correct choice is the one that produces the best overall consequences. Although this premise has an appealing commonsensical ring, it remains deeply controversial among moral philosophers. In the example just mentioned, consequentialists might argue that the action is clearly justified, since saving the life of the older child has enormous value while the costs to the new baby of donating bone marrow are negligible. Moral traditionalists might counter that the same action is clearly unacceptable, because it violates the principle that people shouldn't be used as means for others' ends.

Critics of consequentialist theories attempt to buttress their case by constructing examples in which the choice that consequentialism seems to prescribe strongly violates commonly held moral intuitions. Consider, for example, the following variant of the philosopher's trolley-car problem. A conductor of a trolley sees two strangers standing on the track just ahead, too close for him to be able to stop before running over them. He does have time, however, to divert the car onto a side track. The problem is that doing so will result in the death of a close friend who happens to be standing on that track. Consequentialism seems to require that the conductor divert the car, killing his close friend, since he has every reason to believe that the loss from the two deaths on the main track would outweigh the loss from the death of his friend.

People uncomfortable with that prescription may view it as grounds for rejecting consequentialism as moral theory. Many consequentialists would respond that it is the moral intuition rather than their theory that merits re-examination. But because most people are unwilling to abandon the intuition that killing a close friend is wrong in this case, the debate usually goes no further. In the process, consequentialist moral theories that might be enormously helpful in grappling with emerging ethical questions have lost standing in the minds of many.

The adaptive rationality framework suggests a way around this impasse. In place of the narrow utility function employed in traditional self-interest theory, suppose we assume that most people have the broader range of concerns suggested by the adaptive rationality framework. That is, suppose people care not just about how many deaths an action will cause, but also about the identities of those who will be killed and their relationships to the person who must decide what to do. This step permits us to include in the cost-benefit calculus the fact that both the conductor himself and those who would subsequently learn of the decision he faced would suffer an enormous loss if he were to take an action that resulted in the death of his friend. Such losses might easily be of sufficient magnitude to sustain the intuition that it would be morally acceptable for the conductor to spare his friend's life.

If a proponent of the present-aim standard of rationality offered this argument, she would be vulnerable to the charge of having added an arbitrary taste just to validate the moral intuition that failing to save the friend was unacceptable. A proponent of the adaptive rationality standard can respond to that charge by describing evidence that people with the capacity to develop deep bonds of friendship are for that reason better equipped than others to solve a variety of commitment problems. If their loyalty to their friends is to serve that purpose, however, it must not be something they can suppress at will. (If they could, then there would be no way to distinguish people who were trustworthy from those who were not, which would render trustworthiness useless for solving commitment problems.)

The adaptive rationality framework thus helps sustain a consequentialist account for why it might be morally acceptable to sacrifice two strangers to prevent the death of a close friend. This account concedes that two lives count for more than one, but stresses that the number of lives saved is not the only relevant consequence. Without deep emotional attachments to others, people cannot hope to function effectively. In any serious effort to determine whether an action is morally right, we must consider not just how many people are affected by it, but also who is affected and how.

In confronting many of the emerging ethical dilemmas in the medical domain, traditional moral theories are unlikely to provide useful guidance. In such cases, consequentialist moral reasoning is likely to be the best tool at our disposal, if only because it is the only tool. It can become a much more valuable tool in these contexts if we are careful not to take too narrow a view of the consequences of actions.

Concluding Remarks

Conceptions of rationality and morality have important practical consequences. The functional role of human drives of a narrow biological sort and, more broadly, of preferences and belief systems is to motivate suites of adaptive behaviors. People can exercise at least a limited range of choice about which goals to pursue or which belief systems to adopt. In purely pragmatic terms, the adaptive rationality standard has much to commend it over the self-interest and present-aim standards of rationality.

Unlike the present-aim standard, it does not leave investigators vulnerable to the crankcase-oil objection. On the contrary, it provides us with a disciplined framework for evaluating whether a given preference or goal is a proper basis for explaining and predicting behavior: If the preference or goal promotes, or at least does not hamper, the individual's ability to acquire and hold resources, it may be included; otherwise, not.

Another advantage is that, by showing that the willingness to put community interests ahead of one's own interests can often help a person solve commitment problems, the adaptive rationality standard helps establish that morality — defined as a willingness to put community interests ahead of one's own at least some of the time — is not only consistent with individual survival but often even conducive to it. People want to think of themselves as rational, and they also want to think of themselves as moral. Under the self-interest standard of rationality, the only way this can be accomplished is by adopting what amount to empty conceptions of either interest or morality. By contrast, the adaptive rationality standard makes clear that morality is not only consistent with rationality but, under some conditions, even required by it.

At the same time, the adaptive rationality standard does not encourage the naïve view that community interests and individual interests are always one and the same. On the contrary, it stresses that there will always be at least some tension between these two levels in environments in which individual predispositions are costly to assess. Thus, although the adaptive rationality standard is in several respects a step forward from the present-aim and self-interest standards, it also makes clear that rationality and morality are concepts that inescapably entail at least some ambiguity.

4

Can Socially Responsible Firms Survive
in Competitive Environments?

IN HIS CELEBRATED 1970 ARTICLE, Milton Friedman wrote that "there is one and only one social responsibility of business — to use its resources and engage in activities designed to increase its profits so long as it stays within the rules of the game, which is to say, engages in open and free competition without deception or fraud." In Friedman's view, managers who pursue broader social goals — say, by adopting more stringent emissions standards than required by law or by donating corporate funds to charitable organizations — are simply spending other people's money. Firms run by these managers will have higher costs than those run by managers whose goal is to maximize shareholder wealth. According to the standard theory of competitive markets, the latter firms will attract more capital and eventually drive the former firms out of business.

Of course, as Friedman himself clearly recognizes, there are many circumstances in which the firm's narrow interests coincide with those of the broader community. He writes, for example, that "it may well be in the long-run interest of a corporation that is a major employer in a small community to devote resources to providing amenities to that community or to improving its government. That may make it easier to attract desirable employees, it may reduce the wage bill or lessen losses from pilferage and sabotage or have other worthwhile effects" (1970, 24).

Friedman argues against using the term "social responsibility" to characterize those activities of a firm that, while serving the broader community, also augment the firm's profits. He believes that this language has great potential to mislead politicians and voters about the proper role of the corporation in society, and will foster excessive regulation.

In the years since Friedman wrote, the development of the theory of repeated games has given us ever more sophisticated accounts of the forces that often align self-interest with the interests of others. For example, Robert Axelrod suggests that firms pay their suppliers not because they feel a moral obligation to do so, but because they require future shipments from them (1984, 59).

Repeated interactions clearly often do give rise to behaviors that smack of social responsibility. Yet as Friedman suggests, it is erroneous — or at least misleading — to call these behaviors morally praiseworthy. After all, even a firm whose owners and managers had no concern about the welfare of the broader community would have ample motive to engage in them. When material incentives favor cooperation, it is more descriptive to call the cooperating parties "prudent" than "socially responsible."

It is also an error to assume that repeated interactions always provide ready solutions to social dilemmas and other collective action problems. Even among parties who deal with one another repeatedly, one-shot dilemmas — opportunities for cheating and other opportunistic behavior — often arise. Even a long-standing client of a law firm, for example, has no way to verify that it is billed for only the number of hours actually worked.

In many cases, the knowledge that opportunities to cheat will arise may preclude otherwise profitable business ventures. Consider a person whose mutual fund has just been taken over by new management. She wants advice about whether to stay with the fund under its new management or switch to a different fund. Because there are many stockbrokers who are well acquainted with the available alternatives, the possibility for a mutually beneficial sale of advice clearly exists. Yet the investor also knows that a broker's interests may differ from her own. Perhaps, for example, the broker will receive a large commission or finder's fee if the client switches to a new fund; or perhaps, as was apparently commonplace during the stock market boom of the 1990s, the broker may have recommended specific stocks to curry favor for his firm's investment-banking division. Fearing the consequences of opportunistic behavior, the investor may refrain from seeking advice, in the process depriving both herself and an informed broker of the gains from trade.

When parties to a business transaction confront a one-shot dilemma, their profits will be higher if they defect than if they cooperate. Yet when each party defects, profits for each are lower than if both had cooperated.

In this chapter, I will refer to firms that cooperate in one-shot dilemmas as "socially responsible" firms.

The question I pose is whether such firms can survive in competitive environments. At first glance, it would appear that the answer must be no, for if defecting were indeed a dominant strategy, then socially responsible firms would always have lower returns than pure profit maximizers. But as we saw in chapter 1, cooperation in one-shot dilemmas is sustainable for individuals in competitive environments if certain conditions are met. In this chapter I will suggest that similar conclusions seem to apply in the case of competitive firms.

FIVE WAYS A SOCIALLY RESPONSIBLE FIRM MIGHT PROSPER

The commitment model described in chapter 1 shows how it is possible for cooperative individuals to survive in competitive environments. What does this model have to say about the possibilities for survival of socially responsible firms? The problem confronting such firms is that, by cooperating in one-shot dilemmas, they receive lower payoffs than firms that defect. In the sections below, I will describe five possible avenues along which the socially responsible firm might compensate for that disadvantage. The first three involve the ability to solve commitment problems that arise within and between firms. The last two involve the fact that people value socially responsible action and are willing to pay for it in the marketplace, even when they do not benefit from it directly in a material sense.

Solving Commitment Problems That Arise among Owners, Managers, and Employees

Just as commitment problems arise between independent individuals, so, too, do they arise between owners, managers, and employees. Many of these problems can be solved by mechanisms similar to the ones that work for independent individuals. Some examples follow.

SHIRKING AND OPPORTUNISM. The owner of a business perceives an opportunity to open a branch in a distant city. He knows that if he can hire an honest manager, the branch will be highly profitable. But he cannot monitor the manager, and if the manager cheats the branch will be unprofitable. By cheating, the manager can earn three times as much as he could by being honest. This situation defines a commitment problem. If the owner lacks the ability to identify an honest manager, the venture cannot go forward. But if he has that ability, he can pay the manager well and still earn an attractive return.

PIECE RATES. In cases where individual productivity can be measured with reasonable accuracy, economic theory identifies piece-rate pay schemes as a simple and attractive way to elicit effort from workers. Workers, however, are notoriously suspicious of piece rates. They fear that if they work as hard as they can and do well under an existing piece rate, management will step in and reduce the rate. There is indeed a large literature that describes the elaborate subterfuges employed by workers to prevent this from happening. This literature describes numerous cases in which piece rates were abandoned despite having led to significant increases in productivity. If piece-rate decisions were placed in the hands of someone who had earned the workers' trust, both owners and workers would gain.

CAREER LOCK-IN. Many of the skills one acquires on the job are firm-specific. By accepting long-term employment with a single firm, a worker can thus anticipate that the day will come when her particular mix of skills, although still of value to her employer, will be of relatively little value in the market at large. And with her outside opportunities thus diminished, she will find herself increasingly at her employer's mercy. Firms have a narrow self-interest, of course, in establishing a reputation for treating workers fairly under these circumstances, for this will aid them in their recruiting efforts.

But many workers will find that the firm's self-interest alone may not provide adequate security. A firm may discover, for example, that its employment base will shift overseas during the coming years, and thus stand little to lose by having diminished recruiting ability in the domestic market. Any firm believed to be motivated only by economic self-interest would thus have been at a recruiting disadvantage from the very beginning. By contrast, a firm whose management can persuade workers that fair treatment of workers is a goal valued for its own sake will have its pick of the most able and attractive workers.

RISING WAGE PROFILES. It is a common pattern in industrial pay schemes for pay to rise more rapidly each year than productivity. For this to happen, pay must be less than the value of productivity early in the worker's career, and more than the value of productivity later in his career. There are various reasons offered for this pattern. One is that it discourages shirking, for the worker knows that if he is caught shirking, he may not survive to enjoy the premium pay of the out years. A second rationale is that workers simply like upward-sloping wage profiles. Given a choice between two jobs with the same present value of lifetime income, one with a flat wage profile and the other with a rising profile, most people opt for the second. Whatever the reason for upward-sloping wage profiles, they create an incentive for opportunistic behavior on the part of employers, who stand to gain by firing workers once their wage begins to exceed their productivity. Given the advantages of upward-sloping wage profiles, a firm whose management can be trusted not to renege on its implicit contract stands at a clear advantage.

OTHER IMPLICIT CONTRACTS. A firm with a skilled legal department might be able to devise some formal contractual arrangement whereby it could commit itself not to fire older workers. But such a contract would entail a potentially costly loss of flexibility. No firm can be certain of the future demand for its product, and the time may come when its survival may depend on its ability to reduce its work force. Both the firm and its workers would pay a price if this flexibility were sacrificed.

There are a host of other contingencies that might seriously affect the terms of the bargain between employers and workers. Many of these contingencies are impossible to foresee and hence impossible to resolve in advance by formal contractual arrangements. Any firm whose management can persuade workers that these contingencies will be dealt with in an equitable manner will have a clear advantage in attracting the most able workers.

Solving Commitment Problems with Customers

A variety of commitment problems arise between firms and their customers, and at least some of these are amenable to solution along lines similar to those just discussed. An example follows.

QUALITY ASSURANCE. George Akerlof's celebrated lemons paper (1970) describes a commitment problem in which sellers and buyers alike could benefit if the seller could somehow commit to provide a product or service of high quality. A variety of means have been suggested for solving this problem through reliance on material incentives. Firms can guarantee their products, for example, or they can develop public reputations for supplying high quality (see, for example, Klein and Leffler [1981]).

Yet many forms of the quality-assurance problem cannot be solved by manipulating material incentives. Consider a law firm that could provide the legal services a client wants at a price the client would be willing to pay. But suppose that the client has no way to evaluate the quality of his lawyer's services. There is abundant noise in the legal system, so the outcome of his case by itself is not diagnostic. He might win despite having received shoddy legal help, or he might lose despite having received the best possible help. In such situations, clients are willing to pay premium fees to a firm run by someone they feel they can trust.

Solving Commitment Problems with Other Firms

Commitment problems also arise, finally, in the context of business transactions between firms, and here, too, solutions that rely on character assessment often play a role. Examples follow.

THE SUBCONTRACTOR HOLD-UP PROBLEM. Consider the familiar example of the subcontractor that does most of its business with a single buyer. To serve this buyer at the lowest possible price, much of the subcontractor's human and physical capital would have to be tailored to the buyer's specific needs. Having made those customized investments, however, the subcontractor would then be vulnerable to the "hold-up" problem: Because the buyer knows that the subcontractor's assets cost more than they are worth in the open market, it can pay its subcontractor a price that is above the subcontractor's marginal cost but lower than its average cost. Anticipating this problem, subcontractors will be willing to invest in the capital that best serves their customer's needs only if they believe their partners can be trusted not to exploit them.

In one important study, Edward Lorenz spells out why material incentives are ill-equipped to solve the commitment problems that arise between small French manufacturing firms and their subcontractors. He goes on to describe in detail how parties shop for trustworthy partners. For example, all the respondents in his sample emphasized the heavy weight they placed on personal relationships in this process (Lorenz 1988).

QUALITY ASSURANCE. The problem of quality assurance arises not just between firms and consumers but also in transactions between firms. Consider, for example, the relationship between a parent company and its franchisees. When a franchise owner provides high quality service to the public he enhances not just his own reputation with local buyers but also the reputations of other outlets. The parent firm would like him to take both of these benefits into account in setting his service levels, but his private incentives are to focus only on how good service affects his own buyers. Accordingly, it is common for franchise agreements to call on the franchisee to provide higher-quality service than would otherwise be in his interests to provide. Franchisers incur costs in the attempt to enforce these agreements, but their ability to monitor local service is highly imperfect. The franchiser thus has a strong incentive to recruit franchisees who assign intrinsic value to living up to their service agreements. And the franchisees thus identified are at a competitive advantage over those motivated by self-interest alone.

MAINTAINING CONFIDENTIALITY. Many consulting firms provide services that require access to competitively sensitive information. Clearly no firm could succeed in this line of work if it acquired a reputation for making such information available to its clients' rivals. Yet employees often leave these firms, and when they do their material incentives to maintain confidentiality fall considerably. In some cases, material incentives to maintain confidentiality will be weakened by the fact that multiple parties have had access to the sensitive information, making it much harder to trace the source of any leaks that might occur. With these contingencies in mind, a client would be much more willing to deal with a consulting firm run by someone able to identify and attract employees who assign intrinsic value to honoring confidentiality agreements.

IN THE EXAMPLES JUST DISCUSSED, firms compensate for the higher costs of socially responsible behavior by their ability to solve commitment problems. The next two mechanisms I discuss make use of the observation that social motivations also affect both product demand and labor supply.

The Willingness of Consumers to Support Socially Responsible Firms

The standard free-rider model suggests that buyers will not be willing to pay a premium for products produced by socially responsible firms. For example, consumers may not like the fact that Acme Tire Corporation pollutes the air, but they are said to realize that their own purchase of Acme tires will have a virtually unmeasurable affect on air quality. Accordingly, the theory predicts that if Acme tires sell for even a little less than those produced by a rival with a cleaner technology, consumers will buy from Acme.

Our discussion in chapter 1 challenged this account by explaining how many people might have come to develop a taste for socially responsible behavior. People with such a taste will prefer dealing with socially responsible firms even when they realize that their own purchases are too small to affect the outcomes they care about. Conventional free-rider theory predicted that Star Kist Tuna's sales and profits would fall when it raised its prices to cover the added cost of purchasing only dolphin-safe tuna from suppliers. In the event, however, Star Kist's sales and profits went up, not down. Any consumer who stopped to ponder the matter would know a single household's tuna purchase decision would have no discernible impact on the fate of dolphins. Even so, it appears that many consumers were willing to pay higher prices in the name of a cause they cared about.

There is also evidence that Ben & Jerry's sells more ice cream because of its preservation efforts on behalf of Amazon rain forests; that The Body Shop sells more cosmetics because of its environmentally friendly packaging; that McDonald's sells more hamburgers because of its support for the parents of seriously ill children; and so on.

Experimental evidence from the "dictator game" provides additional evidence of consumers' willingness to incur costs on behalf of moral concerns. The dictator game is played by two players, the first of whom is given a sum of money, say, $20, and is then asked to choose one of two ways of dividing it between himself and the second player: $10 each; or $18 for the first player and $2 for the second. Kahneman, Knetsch, and Thaler (1986) found that more than three-quarters of subjects chose the 10-10 split. They then described this experiment to a separate group of subjects, to whom they then gave a choice between splitting $10 with one of the subjects who had chosen the 10-10 split, or of splitting $12 with one of the subjects who had chosen the 18-2 split. More than 80 percent of these subjects chose the first option, which the authors interpret as a willingness to spend $1 to punish an anonymous stranger who had behaved unfairly in the earlier experiment.

Taken as a whole, the market data and experimental evidence appear to shift the burden of proof to proponents of the free-rider hypothesis.

Ability to Recruit Employees on More Favorable Terms

A fifth and final benefit that accrues to socially responsible firms is the relative advantage they enjoy in recruiting. Jobs differ in countless dimensions, one of which is the degree to which the worker contributes to the well-being of others. If people derive satisfaction from engaging in altruistic behavior, the wages in jobs that afford high levels of moral satisfaction will be significantly lower than the wages paid in jobs otherwise similar. A job applicant can occupy the moral high ground if he wants to, but only by accepting lower wages. And these lower wages, in turn, help offset the higher costs of socially responsible operations.

As we will see in chapter 5, this source of competitive advantage is often large. In a large sample of recent college graduates, for example, those occupying the most desirable jobs on this dimension earned less than half as much as those occupying the least desirable jobs.

CONCLUDING REMARKS

When a business confronts an ethical dilemma, it must incur higher costs if it takes the high road. For example, in the process of refusing to supply master automobile keys to mail-order customers he believes to be car thieves, a locksmith sustains a penalty on the bottom line. Indeed, if the morally preferred action involved no such penalty, there would be no moral dilemmas.

In this chapter, I have described five mechanisms whereby a socially responsible firm might compensate for the higher direct costs of its actions. Three of these involve the ability to solve commitment problems and other one-shot dilemmas. The socially responsible firm is better able than its opportunistic rivals to solve commitment problems that arise between owners, managers, and employees; it is better able to solve commitment problems that arise with customers; and it is better able to solve commitment problems that arise with other firms. A fourth advantage is that buyers are often willing to pay more for the products of socially responsible firms. And finally, the socially responsible firm often enjoys an advantage when recruiting against its less responsible rivals. Taken together, these advantages often appear to be sufficient to offset the higher costs of socially responsible action.

This claim may invite the complaint that what I am calling socially responsible behavior is really just selfishness by another name. Consider, for example, this trenchant commentary by Albert Carr, an economic advisor to Harry Truman:

> The illusion that business can afford to be guided by ethics as conceived in private life is often fostered by speeches and articles containing such phrases as, "It pays to be ethical," or, "Sound ethics is good business." Actually this is not an ethical question at all; it is a self-serving calculation in disguise. The speaker is really saying that in the long run a company can make more money if it does not antagonize competitors, suppliers, employees, and customers by squeezing them too hard. He is

saying that oversharp policies reduce ultimate gains. That is true, but it has nothing to do with ethics. (Carr 1968; reprinted in Donaldson and Werhane 1993, 95)

This line of reasoning implies that any business behavior consistent with survival is selfish by definition. Such a definition, however, is completely at odds with our everyday understanding of the concept. Cooperation in one-shot dilemmas is costly in both the short run and the long run, and for that reason it is properly called unselfish. I have argued that because traits of character are discernible by others, the kinds of people who cooperate in one-shot dilemmas enjoy advantages in other spheres, and these advantages may help them survive in competition with less scrupulous rivals. It simply invites confusion to call the cooperative behaviors themselves self-serving.

Part II

Doing Good

5

What Price the Moral High Ground?

MANY ECONOMISTS ASSUME — implicitly or explicitly — that people are essentially self-interested. Thus, in Gordon Tullock's words, "the average human being is about 95 percent selfish in the narrow sense of the term" (Tullock 1976; quoted in Mansbridge 1990, 12). This approach has generated many powerful insights into human behavior. It explains, for example, why car pools form in the wake of increases in gasoline prices and why the members of "service" organizations are more likely to be real estate salespersons, dentists, chiropractors, insurance agents, and others with something to sell than to be postal employees, truck drivers, or airline pilots.

Yet the assumption of selfishness is not without drawbacks of its own. The most apparent is that, for every behavior that is consistent with this assumption, there seems to be another that contradicts it. A second difficulty with the selfishness assumption is that our models of human behavior appear to mold the behavior of both the modelers themselves and those they teach. Thus, my Cornell colleagues Tom Gilovich and Dennis Regan and I found evidence that people with extensive training in economics are less likely than others to cooperate in social dilemmas, and that this difference is at least in part a consequence of their training. (This evidence is summarized in chapter 9.)

In the end, the importance of other-regarding preferences must be assessed empirically. Here I employ the time-honored tradition of looking to the labor market for evidence on preferences. Just as wage differentials across jobs that carry different levels of risk tell us something about workers' preferences regarding safety, wage differentials in other settings shed light on the strength of our concerns about each other. Indeed, I will argue that, for a large sample of college graduates, even crude measures of the moral satisfaction afforded by different jobs do more to explain wage differences than the human-capital variables traditionally used by economists for this purpose.

A second intriguing finding from the same sample is that measures of moral satisfaction do much to eliminate unexplained wage differentials between men and women. Such differences have always posed a sharp challenge to traditional economic theories of labor markets. These theories lead economists to ask why profit-seeking firms don't rush to hire underpriced women, if, in fact, women are underpaid relative to men. Here I will suggest that one reason women earn lower salaries than comparably qualified men, on average, is that they are more likely than men to choose jobs that afford high measures of moral satisfaction. Such jobs, we will see, pay substantially lower salaries precisely because they offer this desirable attribute. Men who choose these jobs suffer the same wage penalty that women do, but because they choose them less frequently, the average penalty for men is smaller.

EVIDENCE FROM EXISTING STUDIES

The idea that moral concerns might figure in job choices is hardly new. My survey of the existing literature uncovered several sources of evidence — mostly indirect or qualitative — in favor of this hypothesis. One early study, for example, presented the results of a national survey of the factors that influence the career choices of college students. Participants in the survey were asked to "consider to what extent a job or career would have to satisfy each of [the following] requirements before you would consider it IDEAL." (Rosenberg 1957, chap. 11, 12).

1. Provide an opportunity to use my special abilities or aptitudes.
2. Provide me with a chance to earn a great deal of money.
3. Give me a chance to exercise leadership.
4. Give me social status and prestige.
5. Give me an opportunity to work with people rather than things.
6. Enable me to look forward to a stable, secure future.
7. Leave me relatively free of supervision by others.
8. Permit me to be creative and original.

9. Provide me with adventure.

10. Give me an opportunity to be helpful to others.

The most highly ranked of these ten career values was "provide an opportunity to use my special abilities or aptitudes," which was rated as "highly important" by 78 percent of respondents. Next came "enable me to look forward to a stable, secure future" (61 percent), followed by "permit me to be creative and original" (48 percent). The item of special interest for present purposes — "give me an opportunity to be helpful to others" — was ranked fourth on the list of ten. It was rated as highly important by 43 percent of respondents, and another 44 percent called it of "medium importance." Only 13 percent said it was of "little or no importance, irrelevant, or distasteful." Taken at face value, these responses suggest that an overwhelming majority of college students would be willing to trade pay or other desired working conditions in exchange for additional opportunities to help others on the job. These responses, of course, tell us nothing about the rate at which students would be willing to make such tradeoffs.

A second study asked business executives about the effect of their firm's ethical conduct on its profitability (Baumhart 1968). Several respondents said that their firm's ethical posture affected its ability to recruit in the labor market. For instance, an executive of a retail firm whose founder had created a strong reputation for ethical dealing offered this description:

> The top executive has created the kind of environment he wants; it is calculated, but it is good and promotes good ethics. Furthermore, our customers . . . like the courteous and kind treatment given by our sales people. Now we get sales ladies from the same pool of personnel that other retail stores in the area get their help, but our help is more courteous because of the reputation which the president has established. New sales ladies catch on; their better side shows through in their work. *And we don't pay any more than other stores around here either — probably we pay a little less.* (Baumhart 1968, 105; emphasis added)

Other executives reported that a firm's reputation for unethical dealings — even when based on behavior in the distant past — made recruiting more difficult. As one railroad executive put it, "We still have people around who remember the old robber barons. . . . These men were very unethical at the time and the result of their operation still hurts us today" (Baumhart 1968, 107). The same sentiment was echoed by an executive in the electrical industry in reference to that industry's highly publicized price-fixing scandal: "The students really quiz us since the indictments. They want to know whether collusion has stopped and what the company policy is" (Baumhart 1968, 107). Again, while such responses are suggestive, they tell us little about the rate at which workers are willing to trade pay for a working environment that emphasizes social responsibility.

Yet another study surveyed managers in the management information systems (MIS) field to discover the extent to which the ethical posture of their employers was related to job satisfaction (Vitell and Davis 1990). Job satisfaction was assessed using the Managerial Job Satisfaction Questionnaire developed by Cellucci and DeVries (1978). The ethical posture of the respondents' employers was measured by the extent to which respondents agreed with the statement, "MIS managers in my company often engage in behavior that I consider to be unethical." The correlation coefficient between responses to this statement and the index of job satisfaction was -0.26.[1]

As in the case of the other studies reported, this finding suggests a willingness on the part of employees to trade pay and other valued working conditions in exchange for a more ethical working environment. But here again the authors have no basis upon which to estimate the rate at which such job characteristics might be exchanged. This issue is my focus in the remainder of this chapter.

THE THEORETICAL FRAMEWORK FOR THE CURRENT STUDY

Jobs differ in countless dimensions, one of which is the degree to which workers contribute to the well-being of others. Consider two jobs that are identical along all dimensions except this one. (For example, one job might involve writing advertising copy for a product known to cause serious health problems, while the other involves writing advertising copy for the United Way.) If people derive satisfaction from engaging in socially responsible behavior and if the wages in these two jobs were the same, there would be an excess supply of applicants to the second job and a shortage of applicants to the first. In equilibrium, we would therefore expect the less socially desirable job to offer higher pay. A job applicant can occupy the moral high ground if he wants to, but only by accepting lower wages. This wage differential provides a concrete estimate of how strongly the worker cares about the well-being of others.

The practical difficulty is that we rarely find two jobs that are completely alike in all respects except for the extent to which applicants regard them as morally satisfying. When the wages of two jobs differ, a host of other important factors are usually involved, as well — most notably, their respective skill requirements and working conditions unrelated to moral satisfaction. To estimate how much of an observed wage differential between two jobs is accounted for by a difference in perceived social responsibility, we must not only construct an operational measure of the extent to which specific jobs are viewed as morally satisfying, but must also control for individual differences in ability and for differences in other working conditions across jobs.

The ideal way to control for ability is to work with longitudinal data sets — surveys that record the labor-market experiences of individual workers over time. Such data allow us to observe what happens when someone leaves a morally satisfying job for an otherwise similar job that she finds less satisfying in this respect. In such cases, we can be sure that an underlying ability difference does not lie behind any observed change in wages, since the worker in question is the same in both cases. The difficulty with existing longitudinal data sets (such as the National Longitudinal Survey) is that they do not supply sufficiently detailed employer and job descriptions to facilitate measures of moral satisfaction in the workplace.

In cross-section data, the best way to control for ability is to employ standard human-capital measures — quantitative measures of the various factors that influence worker productivity, such as education, experience, training, and the like. The difficulty with most readily available data sets is that the human capital information they provide lacks the rich detail one would ideally like to have for this kind of application. I was therefore fortunate to gain access to a data set that is much richer than most in this regard.

RESULTS FROM THE CORNELL EMPLOYMENT SURVEY

In the late 1980s, Cornell University's career center completed an employment survey of recent graduates of the university's College of Arts and Sciences. This survey provided information on the current activities of respondents nine months after their graduation. For those who were gainfully employed, the survey recorded information on annual salary, job title, and the name and location of employer. Taking special steps to protect the anonymity of respondents, I was able to match the individual survey response forms with the college transcript of each respondent. Thus, unlike standard employment-survey data sets, my data made it possible to control for the respondent's degree field as well as a rich variety of other details related to academic performance. And since almost all of these data pertained to first jobs, I had access to almost as much information as did the employers who did the actual hiring.

By examining annual reports and other available records for each employer represented in the survey, I was able to categorize each employer as belonging to either the profit, nonprofit, or government sector of the economy. These categories provided at least a crude measure of the degree of social responsibility associated with respondents' jobs, with employment in the nonprofit sector rated highest, government next, and the for-profit sector last on the social-responsibility scale. The point is not that work in the for-profit sector carries any presumption of being morally noxious; rather, it is that survey respondents consistently rate jobs in the nonprofit sector as more satisfying in moral terms than otherwise similar jobs in the for-profit sector. (More on this point below.)

One of the most striking patterns in the Cornell survey was the size of the average wage differentials among these employment sectors: An employee in the for-profit sector, for example, earned almost 21 percent more than a government worker, while an employee in the private nonprofit sector earned more than 32 percent less than a government worker. For the sample as a whole, males earned almost 14 percent more than females, but this difference shrank to 11 percent when account was taken of the worker's sector of employment.

Wage differentials across the three broad employment sectors shrank slightly when account was taken of more detailed employee characteristics. Graduates earned 5.3 percent more for each additional mathematics course taken, and 1.5 percent more for each additional economics course, and 3.7 percent more for each business course. After controlling for these and other details of each worker's academic experience, employees in the private for-profit sector earned 13.4 percent more than those in the government sector, while employees in the nonprofit sector earned 28.6 percent less than those in the government sector. Controlling for even these crude details of academic experience reduced the wage premium for male employees to just 5.4 percent. This finding lends support to claims that at least part of the observed male-female earnings differential is attributable to differences in the types of courses taken in college.

In one sense, it may seem hardly surprising that nonprofit firms pay lower wages, since the extremely tight budgets of most nonprofits force them to economize at every turn. From the perspective of strict economic theory, however, the price one actually pays should not depend in this fashion on the prices one is able to pay.

The rich, for example, are able to pay more than the poor for goods like salt, yet salt sells for the same price to rich and poor alike. If one type of salt sells for more than another, it must be because buyers consider it more desirable in some way. Likewise, a firm's ability to pay should not affect the salaries it actually does pay. Most members of the Cornell sample who chose nonprofit jobs could easily have found higher-paying employment in the for-profit sector. That they chose otherwise suggests that they assigned significant value to nonwage aspects of employment in the nonprofit sector.

Nor do the Cornell graduates who chose jobs in the nonprofit sector seem to have been generally less able than their classmates who chose jobs in the for-profit sector. For example, sample employees in the nonprofit sector had an overall grade point average of 3.14, as compared with 3.09 for those in the for-profit sector.

By any reasonable standard, the salary gap between for-profit and nonprofit firms in this sample is enormous. Even after controlling for sex, curriculum, and academic performance, employees of for-profit firms in this sample earned roughly 59 percent more, on the average, than employees of nonprofit firms. Of course, the entire gap is not necessarily attributable to compensating differentials for social responsibility in the nonprofit sector. For example, some of the difference may be the result of unmeasured productivity differences between nonprofit and for-profit workers. But given the relative homogeneity of graduating classes at universities like Cornell, and given our ability to control for curriculum and academic performance, it would be difficult to maintain that unmeasured productivity differences could have accounted for a large share of the nonprofit wage deficit. There is certainly no evidence in these data that nonprofit workers were any less motivated or capable as undergraduate students. As noted, nonprofit employees had slightly higher grade point averages than did for-profit employees, and they also took an average of almost five more science courses.

Another possibility is that dimensions of job satisfaction other than social responsibility may differ systematically between the nonprofit and for-profit sectors. At least some of these differences, however, seem to favor the for-profit sector. For example, the average level of office space and other physical amenities in the workplace is higher in the for-profit than in the nonprofit sector, as are travel allowances and other nonsalary compensation items. Such differences suggest that the true compensation gap between nonprofit and for-profit firms may be even larger than suggested by the wage gap just reported.

To generate a more precise measure of the compensating wage differential for social responsibility, it is necessary to make finer distinctions between employers than the crude tripartite division considered thus far. The strategy I chose was to make use of social attitudes regarding the reported occupations and employers of survey respondents. Because my review of the sociological literature revealed only fragmentary usable information on social responsibility ratings by occupational category, and virtually no information on such ratings by category of employer, I found it necessary to devise original surveys to generate this information.

First, I distributed a list of the names of the largest (and hence most easily recognized) employers from the Cornell salary survey to a large class of second-year Cornell MBA students in a business ethics course, and asked each student to rate each of these employers on a 7-point social responsibility scale. On this scale, 1 represented the least socially responsible employer, 7 the most responsible. Second, I compiled a list of the occupations most frequently reported in the Cornell survey and asked the same group of business ethics students to rate these occupations on a similar 7-point scale.

Because different students applied different standards in their responses on these social responsibility surveys, each student's response for each employer and occupation was recalculated as the difference between her actual numerical response for the item and her mean response for all items in that category. For example, if a student rated the occupation of "teacher" as a 5 on the social responsibility scale, and that student's mean response for all occupations was 3.0, then the student's rating for teacher was assigned a numerical value of +2.0. The corresponding ratings for all students were then averaged to generate the overall social attractiveness rating for each occupation and employer category.

The resulting averages for the 141 job titles evaluated ranged from a low of −1.44 ("Stock Broker")[2] to a high of 1.98 ("Teacher"). Selected job titles and their social attractiveness ratings are shown in table 5.1.

The corresponding average social responsibility ratings for 185 employers ranged from a low of −1.45 (the erstwhile Drexel Burnham Lambert) to a high of 2.24 (Andrus Children's Home). Selected employers and their ratings are shown in table 5.2.[5]

The effect of adding these more detailed measures was to increase by roughly 20 percent the proportion of the variance in individual salaries that could be explained for this sample. The effects of the specific social responsibility variables are shown in figure 5.1. In the top panel we see, for example, that employees with an occupational sociability rating (OSR) greater than +1 earned almost 30 percent less than did otherwise similar workers whose OSR ratings fell between −0.5 and +0.5. Those in the occupations rated least socially responsible (OSR < −1) earned almost 14 percent more than those in the middle category.

The estimates for the Employer Social Responsibility (ESR) variables were less extreme (bottom panel of figure 5.1), but here, too, the salary differential between categories at the opposite end of the spectrum was both large and statistically significant, even after controlling for broad employment sector (nonprofit, government, or for-profit).

Another effect of the inclusion of the occupational and employer social responsibility measures was to reduce the estimated wage premium

TABLE 5.1
Social Responsibility Ratings of Selected Occupations

Occupation	Rating	Occupation	Rating
Stock Broker	−1.44	Military Officer	.49
Salesman	−1.27	Quality-Control Assistant	.50
Trader	−1.14	Reporter	.57
Expatriate Tax Specialist	−1.03	Physicist	.60
Leasing Consultant	−.90	Librarian	.62
Buyer	−.66	Emergency Room Registrar	.69
Account Officer	−.63	Park Ranger/Interpreter	.72
Marketing Analyst	−.60	Geologist	.73
Tax Associate	−.58	Chemist	.87
Advertising Coordinator	−.57	Nurse's Assistant	.87
Risk Analyst	−.50	Nanny	.92
Publicist	−.48	Agro-Forester	1.14
Credit Analyst	−.42	Counselor	1.18
Appraiser	−.32	Family Advocate	1.21
Accountant	−.16	Child Behavior Specialist	1.53
Mathematician	−.06	Environmental Consultant	1.66
Congressional Intern	.01	Child Care Counselor	1.78
Legislative Analyst	.05	Community Health Worker	1.82
Intern	.18	Substance Abuse Prevention	1.84
Foreign Service Officer	.20	Shelter Coordinator	1.89
Archaeological Supervisor	.34	Emergency Medical Technician	1.98
Engineer	.45	Teacher	1.98

for males to just 3.5 percent, a difference that is not statistically significant at conventional levels. The kinds of courses people take influence wages, as do the kinds of jobs they choose. When males chose jobs deemed to afford high levels of moral satisfaction, they suffered the same reduction in pay that women did. But men were much less likely to have chosen such jobs in the first place. For the Cornell sample, at least, sex appears to have had essentially no independent influence on wages.

Again, these estimates of compensating differentials for social responsibility are remarkably large. They are based on fragmentary measures of occupational and employer social responsibility and should for this rea-

TABLE 5.2
Social Responsibility Ratings for Selected Employers

Employer	Rating	Employer	Rating
Drexel Burnham Lambert	−1.45	AT&T	.27
Salomon Brothers	−1.18	DuPont	.33
BBDO	−.74	Xerox	.45
Covington & Burling	−.62	Hewlett Packard	.47
E. F. Hutton	−.59	Carnation Company	.49
Cravath, Swaine & Moore	−.59	New American Library	.59
New Horizons Motion		McGraw-Hill Inc.	.69
Picture	−.47	Hoffman-La Roche	.71
Macy's	−.38	The Buffalo News	.72
Ratner Kessler Realty	−.35	U.S. News & World Report	.89
Arthur Andersen & Co.	−.30	W. W. Norton and Co.	.97
General Dynamics	−.29	Scientific American	1.05
Metropolitan Life	−.16	The Chronicle of Higher	
Holiday Inns Inc.	−.03	Education	1.14
Data General Corp.	−.01	Bristol-Myers Squibb	1.25
Prudential Insurance	−.01	Oncogene Sciences	1.29
Digital equipment	.016	New England Journal of	
IBM	.09	Medicine	1.67
Aetna Life & Casualty Co.	.13	Boston City Hospital	2.13
		Andrus Children's Home	2.24

son be regarded as tentative. But as we will see, they are broadly consistent with evidence from a variety of alternative sources.

SALARY DIFFERENTIALS BETWEEN CORPORATE AND PUBLIC INTEREST LAW

Another source of evidence on the strength of unselfish motives comes from salary differentials between public interest lawyers and corporate lawyers. When the public interest law movement expanded rapidly in the 1960s, the salary differences between public interest lawyers and other attorneys were small, on the order of only a few thousand dollars per year. In the intervening years, however, public interest law salaries rose only modestly while compensation in other areas of the law mush-

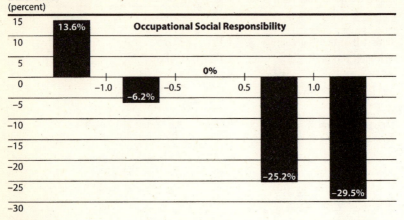

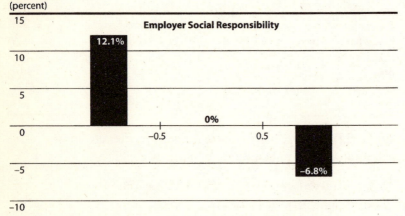

Figure 5.1 Compensating Salary Differentials for Social Responsibility

roomed sharply. By the late 1980s the gap between public interest and other legal salaries had grown extremely large. Thus, the average starting salary for public interest lawyers in 1987 was only $23,843, as compared to $39,847 for all other lawyers in their first year of private practice (Studley 1989, 18).[4]

The gap between starting salaries for public interest lawyers and first-

TABLE 5.3
1989 Starting Salaries for Private and Public Interest Lawyers

First-Year Public Interest Lawyers	First-Year Associates in Private Law Firms
American Civil Liberties Union New York: $28,000	Millbank, Tweed, Hadley & McCoy New York: $83,000
Center for Constitutional Rights New York: $29,000	Skadden, Arps, Slate, Meagher & Flom New York: $83,000
People for the American Way Washington, D.C.: $25,000	Arent, Fox, Kintner, Plotkin & Kahn Washington, D.C.: $66,000
Public Citizen Litigation Group Washington, D.C.: $21,000	Dow, Lohnes & Albertson Washington, D.C.: $67,000

Source: *National Law Journal*, 26 March 1990.

year associates in private law firms was even larger. Table 5.3 presents 1989 starting salaries for a small sample of institutions in these two categories.

As with the earlier effort to account for salary differences among Cornell graduates, the main problem here, too, is to discover the extent to which differences in law salaries may simply reflect unmeasured differences in productivity. There is some evidence that the lawyers who choose employment in small public interest organizations in isolated locations may indeed have less formidable academic credentials than their counterparts in large urban law firms, but the same can also be said of attorneys who work in small, isolated, private law firms. There is apparently a surfeit of highly qualified applicants for each position in well located, highly visible public interest groups, such as the Natural Resources Defense Council and American Civil Liberties Union in New York City. Writing in the *National Law Journal*, a trade newspaper for the legal profession, Jamienne Studley reported that "well-known policy and advocacy organizations are typically deluged with excellent applicants" (Studley 1989, 16). Indeed, such groups are often able to attract law review graduates from the nation's elite law schools, people who could have had their pick from among the most highly sought entry-level jobs in the legal profession. Even so, the starting salary for an attorney for the New York ACLU in 1989 was only $28,000, as compared with an average of $83,000 for first-year attorneys in a sample of large New York law firms surveyed by *The National Law Journal* (26 March 1990, s3).

Published commentary in the legal trade press explicitly acknowledges the link between the lower pay of public interest jobs, on the one hand, and the desire to perform socially beneficial work, on the other. For example, Douglas Phelps, executive director of the Massachusetts Public Interest Research Group and former director of the Public Interest Placement and Career Development Office at Harvard Law School, wrote that students "get paid sixty thousand dollars for doing what they don't believe in versus fifteen thousand dollars for doing what they do believe in" (quoted by Miller [1987, 27]). There is also evidence that if the pay gap between public interest law and the rest of the profession were smaller, the demand for public interest positions would be much more intense. A fellowship program sponsored by a leading Wall Street law firm that augmented starting salaries in public interest law produced a flood of applicants: "The experience of the new Skadden Fellowships confirms new graduates' intense desire for public interest jobs: More than 600 outstanding beginning lawyers applied for 25 public interest awards that would pay generously for the public sector but well below law firm or even average lawyer starting levels" (Studley 1989, 16).

Private law firms themselves seemed to appreciate the strength of the latent demand for a more socially responsible dimension to legal employment, and some took concrete steps to incorporate opportunities for public interest work in their own positions. In the spring of 1987, for example, seventeen law firms announced plans to furlough their incoming associates to work for the summer in public interest law agencies "while the firms paid the associates their full salary for ten weeks" (Miller 1987, 28). The firms taking this step were said to view it as an investment in recruitment. According to Sally Hancock, executive director of Public Interest Law Internship, a Chicago-based group that provides summer internships at public interest organizations, "It markets the law firm as one that has an interest in humanity and therefore is humane. It helps them in recruitment" (quoted by Miller [1987, 28]).

Fees for Expert-Witness Testimony

During the past several decades, hearings in Congress have explored public policy issues related to tobacco smoke. Many of the early hearings focused on whether people who smoke cigarettes are more likely than others to contract various pulmonary and cardiovascular diseases. Subsequent hearings focused on whether exposure to "secondhand" smoke in the environment is a public health hazard. Throughout these hearings, there was a common pattern of expert-witness testimony. On one side, witnesses associated with the American Cancer Society, the American Heart Association, the American Lung Association, and other public interest groups testified to the effect that tobacco smoke was a significant causal factor in the health problems at issue. On the opposing side, witnesses sponsored by the Tobacco Institute and other industry groups testified to the effect that the health risks associated with tobacco smoke were either unproved or highly exaggerated. Since 1964, when the first Surgeon General's report appeared identifying cigarette smoke as a major public health hazard, there had been a growing perception that advocates of the industry's position in these hearings are morally suspect. By now it seems fair to say that a large percentage of the population shares the perception that witnesses for the public interest groups occupy the moral high ground in the tobacco hearings.

For the purposes of the present study, the question is whether the compensation differentials for the expert witnesses associated with the two sides reflect this perception. In 1967, Senator Daniel Brewster (D, MD) attempted to answer this question by contacting witnesses who had appeared before, or submitted statements to, the Senate Commerce Committee's 1965 hearings on regulating tobacco smoking. Brewster discovered that witnesses favoring cigarette regulation generally appeared as unpaid volunteers. Many pro-industry witnesses refused to discuss their compensation arrangements, but five admitted that they had appeared in return for financial payments from either the industry itself or law firms representing it (*Business Week*, 9 September 1967).

In an attempt to discover whether this compensation pattern has persisted, I contacted representatives of various public interest groups who sponsor witnesses before congressional tobacco hearings. These groups reported that, almost without exception, their expert witnesses appear without charge, in many cases even paying their own travel expenses. I had much greater difficulty obtaining specific information on the fees paid to experts who testify on behalf of the tobacco industry. Indeed, it is fair to characterize these fees as a carefully guarded industry secret. Almost all unofficial sources, however, reported that industry groups — most notably the Tobacco Institute — compensated their expert witnesses handsomely. One source, a senior scientific research professional formerly associated with the tobacco industry, reported that the current "official" rate for industry expert witnesses was in the range of $200 to $250 per hour. This source, who asked not to be identified, also reported that because the industry had an obvious interest in keeping its official witness fees low, the actual rate of compensation in many cases far exceeded the official hourly rate. The difference was achieved in a variety of ways. I was told, for instance, that witnesses might be paid at the official hourly rate for activities only peripherally related to their testimony — activities such as "keeping up with the literature" or attending professional meetings and conferences. Whatever the total rate of compensation for industry witnesses may have been, it was substantial by any standard, certainly far in excess of the payments received by witnesses who appeared on behalf of public interest groups (which in most cases, again, were zero).

When questioned, tobacco industry sources made no pretense that the higher fees received by their witnesses were necessitated by superior professional credentials. On the contrary, all available evidence suggested that the volunteer witnesses for the public interest groups were much more professionally distinguished than their tobacco industry counterparts. Most members of the volunteer group were active scientific researchers who held faculty positions at prestigious universities and medical schools. Most tobacco industry witnesses, by contrast, described themselves as affiliates of private consulting firms and did not conduct ongoing programs of scientific research. As one former tobacco industry expert witness told me, "At this point, I know of only a few academics who still testify on behalf of the industry. All the others are consultants whose scientific thought process stopped years ago."

Reservation Pay-Premium Survey

The final component of this study is based on a survey of the employment preferences of a sample of Cornell graduating seniors. In this sur-

TABLE 5.4
Six Hypothetical Career Decisions

Ad copywriter for Camel cigarettes		Ad copywriter for the American Cancer Society
Accountant for a large petrochemical company		Accountant for a large art museum
Language teacher for the CIA	or	Language teacher for a local high school
Recruiter for Exxon		Recruiter for the Peace Corps
Lawyer for the National Rifle Association		Lawyer for the Sierra Club
Chemist for Union Carbide		Chemist for Dow Chemical

vey, students were asked to consider six pairs of hypothetical job descriptions. Within each pair, pay, working conditions, and the specific tasks involved were described as being essentially the same, but the social responsibility rating of each employer differed (e.g., "write advertisements for the American Cancer Society" versus "write advertisements for Camel cigarettes").[5] The six pairs of jobs are listed in table 5.4.

Subjects were first asked which of the two jobs in each pair they would choose if each paid a salary of $30,000 per year. They were then asked how much higher the salary would have had to be in the job not chosen in order for them to have reversed their decision. As expected, the overwhelming majority of subjects indicated a preference for the jobs in the right column of table 5.4.[6] The proportions choosing these jobs, and the average and median pay premiums required for switching are reported in table 5.5.

The median pay premium for switching jobs was by far the smallest for the sixth pair of jobs — chemist for Dow Chemical/chemist for Union Carbide. Two factors may help explain why students perceived any difference at all between these ostensibly equivalent jobs. First, the large volume of negative publicity surrounding the Bhopal disaster in India, which was still being widely discussed at the time of this survey, may have sullied Union Carbide's reputation in the minds of many students. And second, Dow had invested heavily during that era in an advertising campaign touting the many socially responsible endeavors in which its employees were engaged. It is interesting to note that in the late 1960s and early 1970s, the perceptions of these two companies were likely re-

TABLE 5.5
Reservation Pay Premiums for Sacrificing the Moral High Ground

Employer	Percent choosing	Median pay premium for switching	Average premium for switching
American Cancer Soc.	88.2	$15,000/yr	$24,333/yr
Art Museum	79.4	$5,000/yr	$14,185/yr
High School	82.4	$8,000/yr	$18,679/yr
Peace Corps	79.4	$5,000/yr	$13,037/yr
Sierra Club	94.1	$10,000/yr	$37,129/yr*
Dow Chemical	79.4	$2,000/yr	$11,796/yr

*Excludes one response of $1,000,000,000,000,000/yr.

versed. Dow was at that time under heavy criticism for its manufacture of napalm, which was being dropped by American bombers on the villages of Vietnam.

The largest median reservation pay premium for switching jobs — $15,000 per year — obtained for the first pair (ad copywriter for Camel cigarettes versus ad copywriter for the American Cancer Society). Students also reported large reservation pay premiums for the fifth pair of jobs — lawyer for the National Rifle Association (NRA) and lawyer for the Sierra Club. The median respondent required $10,000 per year more in salary to switch from the Sierra Club to the NRA, while the average reservation pay premium reported for the same move was more than $37,000 per year.

The reservation pay premiums reported by these subjects are large by almost any standard. Of course, it is hard to know whether subjects would really require premiums this large when confronted with an actual opportunity to switch to a less morally attractive, but higher paying, job. It is possible, for example, that people might report high premiums when asked to consider such job changes in the abstract, and yet be willing to switch for significantly smaller amounts when confronted with the reality of personal budget problems. Bear in mind, though, that we saw compensating differentials on an even larger scale in the case of public interest lawyers and their counterparts in private law firms. And even if the actual reservation premiums were only one tenth as large as the ones reported by our survey respondents, they would still constitute a highly significant feature of the contemporary labor market.

The survey results reported in this section help supplement the earlier findings in two important ways. First, because the sample of students was randomly chosen, the problem of unobserved differences in individual productivity is no longer an issue. (Recall that the earlier Cornell survey suffered from this problem because it consisted of people who had already segregated themselves into different categories of employment.) A second problem with the earlier Cornell survey involved the effect of differing attitudes about social responsibility. If people's feelings about this issue differed substantially, then the observed wage premium for socially irresponsible tasks would tend to understate the compensation required by the average person to perform such tasks. In the limiting case, if there were sufficiently many people who didn't care at all about whether they performed socially responsible tasks, we would observe no wage premium for the performance of disapproved tasks. The fact the survey reported in this section asked for the reservation wages of a random sample thus helps shed additional light on the population distribution of valuations for socially responsible tasks.

IMPLICATIONS FOR BUSINESS BEHAVIOR

Suppose we accept, for the sake of discussion, that there are significant compensating salary differentials for morally satisfying jobs. This relationship has important implications for the behavior of firms with respect to a variety of moral and ethical issues. As discussed in the preceding chapter, for example, it challenges the widely held view that the social obligation of a private firm extends no further than to obey the laws of the society in which it operates (again, see Friedman [1970]). The seemingly compelling argument in support of this view is that any business that attempts to exceed this standard is destined to be driven out of business by competitors. This argument fails, however, if there are significant compensating salary differentials for social responsibility in the workplace, for such differentials may often enable firms to withstand the higher costs that would otherwise be associated with acting in a socially responsible manner.

CONCLUDING REMARKS

In this chapter, I have examined the labor market for evidence relevant to the claim that the economic choices of many people are significantly guided by unselfish motives. Earlier studies provided qualitative support for this claim on the basis of survey evidence. One author found that college students listed "helping others" as one of their most important career goals. Another found that executives believed that their firms' ethical posture had a significant impact on their ability to recruit and retain desirable employees. And a survey of executives found a significant negative correlation between job satisfaction and the extent to which respondents felt that other executives in their firm engaged in unethical behavior.

We then saw a variety of evidence for a strong negative correlation between annual earnings, on the one hand, and the degree to which an employee's employer and occupation are viewed as being morally satisfying, on the other. The most systematic of this evidence came from a survey of graduates of Cornell University's College of Arts and Sciences. The same pattern was observed in comparisons of the fees paid to expert witnesses who testify on behalf of the tobacco industry and their counterparts who testify for the American Heart Association and other public interest groups. We also saw dramatic pay differences between public interest lawyers and those employed in other segments of the legal profession. And we saw survey evidence from a sample of graduating seniors who reported that they would require large premiums before being willing to switch to a less socially responsible employer.

Taken individually, each of these observations is subject to alternative interpretations. Viewed as a whole, however, the evidence paints a picture that is strongly consistent with the claim that unselfish motives figure prominently in economic behavior. It seems fair to conclude that the burden of proof now properly lies on those who claim that economists may safely neglect unselfish motives.

NOTES

1. This correlation was statistically significant at the .05 level.

2. The survey was conducted in 1990, when several major Wall Street scandals were still fresh in memory.

3. There were 134 respondents whose occupational titles were either unavailable or for some other reason were not evaluated in the social responsibility survey. The corresponding figure for employers was 406.

4. See Weisbrod (1983) for additional evidence and interpretation of the salary gap between public interest lawyers and those in private practice. One apparent effect of this growing gap has been a steady reduction in the proportion of law graduates accepting employment in the public interest sector. According to surveys done by the National Association for Law Placement, the percentage of law graduates taking public interest jobs fell from 5.9 percent in 1978 to 3.0 percent in 1986.

5. The exact wording of the instructions to subjects was as follows:

Several pairs of jobs are described on the list below. All of these jobs offer a starting salary of $30,000/year. The jobs in each pair are located in the same city, and both involve working the same number of hours each week. The actual tasks you perform in each job are essentially the same, as are all relevant fringe benefits (pensions, paid vacations, insurance, etc.). The *only real difference* between the jobs in each pair involves the nature of the employer's line of business. In one of the blank spaces provided next to each job, check the member of each pair of jobs that you would accept if you had to choose one or the other. Then in the blank space below the job you did *not* choose, write the minimum annual salary required for you to switch your job choice. To illustrate, suppose that in the first pair of jobs you choose to work for the American Cancer Society when both jobs pay $30,000/year. You should then use the blank space below the Camel cigarettes job to indicate how high its salary would have to be for you to switch. For example, if you say $40,000, that means that if Camel paid $39,999 or less you would still choose the American Cancer Society, but that for $40,000 or more you would choose Camel.

6. On the actual survey form completed by subjects, the more attractive job for a given pair sometimes appeared on the right, sometimes on the left.

6

Local Status, Fairness, and Wage Compression Revisited

NEARLY TWO DECADES ago, I suggested that concerns about relative position might help explain why the distribution of compensation within firms is more compressed than the corresponding distribution of productivity (Frank 1984). In the interim, several other authors have sought to explain the same phenomenon by reference to concerns about equity or fairness. In this chapter, I examine some of the strengths and weaknesses of these competing explanations.

THE ANOMALY OF PAY COMPRESSION

Standard models of competitive wage determination tell us that the distribution of compensation within a firm will closely mimic the distribution of its workers' marginal productivities. And yet for those firms for which available data facilitate the relevant comparisons, individual differences in pay appear to sharply understate individual variations in productivity.

In my earlier work, I attempted to persuade academic readers of the plausibility of this claim by suggesting the following thought experiment: First, identify the two professors in your department whose overall contribution to your department's mission is more valuable than that of any other two in the same age group. Next, identify the three professors from the same age group whose overall contribution is least valuable. Then answer this question: If both groups were to leave, which one's absence would hurt more? Most people quickly indicate a preference to keep the two best professors. If workers are paid their marginal products, we should then expect the combined salaries of the two best professors to exceed the combined salaries of the three worst. Yet typically we see just the reverse. In most departments, the combined salaries of *any* two professors in a given age group come to less than the combined salaries of any other three.

Similar pay compression is observed in industrial firms, where salaries are typically set by administrative formulas based on education, experience, seniority, and various job characteristics. The use of these formulas simplifies the task of pay administrators, yet there is little doubt that individual differences in productivity are often demonstrably greater than the resulting differences in pay.

In principle, pay compression might be accounted for by a variety of factors that are consistent with a narrow interpretation of the neoclassical labor-market model. In a world of incomplete information, for example, risk-averse workers might find contracts attractive in which firms promised to pay them their expected marginal products, thus guarding against the possibility of having to work for extremely low wages in the event that subsequent experience revealed them to be unproductive. This account appears plausible, since we know that people tend to be highly risk averse with respect to many other gambles with high stakes. The practical difficulty, however, is that labor contracts do not permit the degree of commitment necessary to prevent the most productive workers from being bid away by other firms. And unless a firm could assure that its most productive workers would stay on under the terms of the original contract, it could not promise to subsidize its least productive workers under that contract.

Another possibility is that pay differences may understate productivity differences because managers are simply unable to measure productivity differences with any precision. This account also has face validity. After all, work is often performed in large, complex teams, making it exceedingly difficult to assess individual contributions. Yet if measurement were the only difficulty, there would be no anomaly to explain. The observed distribution of compensation within firms poses a puzzle precisely because our ability to assess individual differences in productivity, imperfect though it be, tells us that these differences are much larger than the corresponding differences in pay.

It is this puzzle that both the fairness and local-status models attempt to solve.

PAY COMPRESSION ARISING FROM CONCERNS ABOUT FAIRNESS

The institutional labor literature has long emphasized the importance of concerns about equity in pay determination (see, for example, Belcher and Atchison [1987]). Conspicuous pay differences within groups are said to summon resentment on the part of lesser-paid workers, and a sense of discomfort or embarrassment on the part of those paid the most. Given these reactions to pay inequality, workers will prefer, other things being equal, to work in firms in which pay differences are kept small.

Of course, other things will not be equal in such firms. The least productive workers in such a firm would benefit not only from the good feelings engendered by pay equity, but also from an absolute increase in pay. The most productive workers in such firms, by contrast, would enjoy only the former benefit. Relative to a scheme in which workers are paid their marginal products, these workers would experience an absolute cut in pay. But if we assume that they, too, value the harmony that accompanies pay equity, then at least some financial sacrifice may seem justified to them on this account.

More recent papers in the fairness literature have emphasized that negative feelings may not be the only consequence of conspicuous pay inequality; the resulting decline in morale may also take a toll on productivity (Akerlof and Yellen 1986; Levine 1991; Romer 1992). On this view, there is still another reason for workers to prefer firms that provide at least a modicum of pay equity. Relative to the case in which all workers are paid their respective marginal products, a more compressed wage schedule may enable *all* workers to earn absolutely higher wages. This would happen, for example, if the surplus resulting from pay compression were distributed in inverse proportion to productivity.

Although many economists appear reluctant to introduce concerns about fairness into models of competitive labor-market behavior, there is growing evidence that such concerns motivate costly actions for many people. Werner Guth, Rolf Schmittberger, and Bernd Schwarze, for example, have demonstrated the strength of such concerns in a series of experimental two-player games (1982). In those experiments, the first player (Proposer) proposes how a given sum of money will be divided between himself and the second player (Responder), whereupon each gets the amount proposed if Responder accepts, but each gets zero if Responder refuses. Because of its take-it-or-leave-it nature, this game is called "the ultimatum bargaining game." One-sided offers in these experiments were rare, and the most common proposal was for a 50–50 split.

Did most Proposers in these experiments avoid one-sided offers in the interests of fair play, or merely because they feared responders might reject such proposals? Kahneman, Knetsch, and Thaler (1986) explored this question by giving subjects an opportunity to participate in the dictator game, discussed in chapter 4. In that game, recall, subjects were asked to allocate $20 between themselves and another subject in either of two ways: by splitting the money evenly; or by keeping $18 for themselves and giving only $2 to the other subject. More than three-fourths of subjects chose the 50–50 split, suggesting a fairness motive for the pattern of original offers in Guth's experiments.

Recall also that in their follow-up experiment, Kahneman, Knetch, and Thaler found that subjects were willing to incur costs in order to "punish" subjects who had chosen the one-sided split in the earlier experiment. Thus, when the follow-up subjects were given a choice between splitting $10 evenly with those who had chosen the even split in the earlier experiment or splitting $12 evenly with those who had chosen the one-sided split, more than 80 percent chose the former.

The amounts involved in these experiments were not large, and skeptics may question whether people are willing to incur more substantial losses in the name of fairness. There is at least fragmentary evidence that many often are, as in labor disputes in which employees commit themselves to positions that seem overwhelmingly likely to reduce their future incomes. Arguing that the terms of their existing contract were grossly unfair, for example, pilots for the former Eastern Airlines went out on strike despite credible indications that doing so would cost them their jobs.

Although we have much more to learn about the extent to which people are willing to incur costs in the name of fairness, existing evidence leaves little doubt that most people are willing to incur such costs. And to the extent that most people associate greater pay compression with greater fairness, it then follows that concerns about fairness could motivate the choice of employment under a compressed wage structure, even by a high-ranking employee who would be relatively disadvantaged under such a structure.

PAY COMPRESSION ARISING FROM CONCERNS ABOUT LOCAL STATUS

The mechanism whereby concerns about local status translate into wage compression is straightforward. It begins with the assumption that workers value local status, which for present purposes I define as their rank vis-à-vis their co-workers in their firm's pay distribution. It also assumes that employees cannot be forced to remain with a firm against their wishes. These two assumptions imply that there can be no equilibrium in which workers of unequal productivity in a firm are paid the respective values of their marginal products. To see why, suppose there were such a firm. Workers in the bottom of its pay distribution could then leave and form a new firm consisting only of workers whose productivities were equal to their own, thereby escaping the burden of low status. If firms paid each worker exactly the value of her marginal product, the only stable outcome would be for each firm to consist of workers with the same level of productivity.

Local status is a reciprocal phenomenon. High-status positions, and the satisfaction that derives from them, cannot exist unless they occur in tandem with positions of low status. So although low-ranking workers gain when they leave a firm that pays them only their marginal products, their absence imposes a cost on the formerly high-ranking workers in the abandoned firm.

If high local status is a normal good — that is, if the amount people are willing to pay for it rises with income — then the gain to the low-ranking workers who leave will be smaller than the corresponding loss to their high-ranking colleagues who remain. Both groups can thus be made better off if the high-ranking workers compensate the low-ranking workers to remain. This is, in effect, what happens when the distribution of pay is compressed relative to the corresponding distribution of productivity. Under such a pay schedule, the high-ranking members of any firm may be said to purchase their local status from their less productive co-workers.

Considering the labor market as a whole, those who care least about local status will do best to join firms in which most workers are more productive than themselves. As lesser-ranked members in these firms, they will receive extra compensation. People who care most strongly about rank, by contrast, will choose firms in which most other workers are less productive than themselves. For the privilege of occupying top-ranked positions in those firms, they will have to work for less than the value of what they produce.

Workers are thus able to sort themselves among a hierarchy of firms in accordance with their demands for within-firm status. Figure 6.1 depicts the menu of choices confronting workers whose productivity takes a given value, M. The heavy lines represent the wage schedules offered by three different firms. These schedules tell how much a worker with a given productivity would be paid in each firm. Average productivity is highest in Firm 3, next highest in Firm 2, and lowest in Firm 1. The problem facing persons with productivity level M is to choose which of these three firms for which to work.

Workers who care most about status will want to purchase high-ranked positions like the one labeled A in Firm 1. In such positions, they work for less than the value of what they produce. By contrast, those who care least about status will elect to receive wage premiums by working in lesser-ranked positions like the one labeled C in Firm 3. Workers with moderate concerns about local rank will be attracted to intermediate positions like the one labeled B in Firm 2, for which they neither pay nor receive any compensation for local rank.

Note also in figure 6.1 that even though not every worker in each firm is paid the value of what she produces, workers taken as a group nonetheless do receive the value of what they produce. The extra compensation received by each firm's low-ranking workers is exactly offset by the shortfall in pay of its high-ranking workers.

Conventional neoclassical models of the labor market, by contrast, say that *every* worker is paid the value of what she produces. Yet, as noted at the outset, in every firm and occupation for which the relevant data are available, high-ranking workers are paid less — often substantially less —

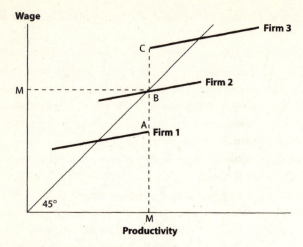

Figure 6.1 The Wage Structure when Local Status Matters

than the value of what they produce, while low-ranking workers are paid more. According to the local-status model, the difference represents a compensating differential for local rank.

Under the adaptive rationality standard discussed in chapter 3, the claim that people have a taste for local status must be supported not only by evidence that many people in fact have such a taste, but also by a plausible showing that persons thus motivated need not be handicapped in their efforts to survive and reproduce in competitive environments. On the first point, survey evidence consistently supports the importance of relative economic position as a determinant of individual well-being. For example, surveys that ask people to report whether they are "very happy," "fairly happy," or "not happy," find that happiness levels within a country at a given moment are strongly positively correlated with position in the country's income distribution (for a summary of the relevant survey evidence, see Frank [1999, chap. 5]; see also Frey and Stutzer, [2002, chap. 4]). The same surveys find no long-term trends in average reported happiness levels, even for countries whose incomes have been growing steadily over time. Looking at different countries at a given point of time, the happiness surveys also find little relationship between the average income level in a country and the average happiness level reported by its citizens.

These findings are thus consistent with the view that relative position is a much more important determinant of self-rated happiness levels than is absolute position on the income scale. Even though happiness surveys call for purely subjective responses, there is evidence that they measure a real phenomenon. For example, numerous other studies have found strong positive relationships between reported happiness levels and observable physiological and behavioral measures of well-being. People who report that they are not happy, for example, are more likely to experience headaches, rapid heartbeat, digestive disorders, and related ailments. Those who rate themselves as very happy are more likely than others to initiate social contacts with friends, less likely to seek psychological counseling, and less likely to attempt suicide. (For a more detailed survey of this evidence, see Frank [1985, chap. 2].)

How does concern about relative position affect survival prospects? If we adopt the evolutionary biologist's view that human motivation was shaped by natural selection in local environments, people would appear to have multiple coherent reasons for this concern. After all, even in a famine there is always *some* food available, and the question of who gets it is settled largely by relative wealth holdings. Concern about relative position may also be adaptive insofar at it prods people to monitor how they are doing relative to their competitors and to boost their effort levels if they start falling behind. The alternative of operating at maximum effort levels at all times is less efficient in that people tend to do better by conserving their energy when environmental conditions are not stressful for use when the threats to survival are more immediate.

Michael McGuire and his collaborators have shown that relative position may even affect fundamental biochemical processes in the nervous system (McGuire, Raleigh, and Brammer 1982; and Raleigh, McGuire, Brammer, and Yuweiler 1984). In a study involving nineteen groups of adult vervet monkeys, McGuire, Raleigh, and Brammer found that the dominant member in each group had concentrations of the neurotransmitter serotonin, which affects mood and behavior in a variety of ways, that were roughly 50 percent higher than those of nondominant members. They also showed that this difference was the effect, rather than the cause, of high local status. To do this, they removed the initially dominant animal from each group and placed him in an isolation cage. Shortly thereafter, a new individual established dominance within each group, and after roughly seventy-two hours passed, serotonin concentrations in the newly dominant animal rose to the levels seen in the formerly dominant animal. At the same time, the serotonin concentrations in the formerly dominant animal fell to the level associated with subordinate status. When the initially dominant animal was returned to the group, he reasserted dominance and serotonin concentrations in both the originally dominant and interim dominant animals responded accordingly.

Within limits, having elevated serotonin concentrations is associated with enhanced feelings of well-being. Serotonin deficiencies are associated with sleep disorders, irritability, and antisocial behavior. McGuire and his colleagues have also found elevated serotonin levels in the leaders of college fraternities and athletic teams.

To sum up, evidence from several disciplines strongly suggests that relative economic position is an important determinant of human satisfaction. There is also persuasive evidence that people are strongly motivated by concerns about fairness. As we have seen, both of these concerns could lead people to prefer pay schemes in which the distribution of individual rewards is more compressed than the corresponding distribution of marginal productivity. By contrast, conventional neoclassical labor-market models, which assume that people care neither about fairness nor about relative economic position, imply pay distributions based strictly on productivity.

Discriminating between the Fairness and Local-Status Models

Wage Compression versus Intensity of Co-Worker Interaction

One testable implication of the local-status model is that wage compression will increase with the degree of interaction among co-workers. After all, even someone who cared a great deal about local status would not

TABLE 6.1
Pay Compression vs. Intensity of Interaction

Occupation	Pay Increase per Additional Dollar of Profit Generated
Research Chemists	<$0.09
Automobile Salespersons	$0.23
Real-estate Agents	$0.50–$0.65

be willing to pay much for a high-ranked position in a group in which co-workers seldom interacted with one another.

In my earlier work, I tested this prediction by looking at how wage compression varied with the intensity of co-worker interaction in a sample of three occupations for which the relevant measures could be constructed (Frank 1984). Research chemists interact more intensively with their co-workers than automobile salespersons do with theirs, and auto salespersons, in turn, interact more intensively than do real estate agents. And as the estimates in table 6.1 indicate, I found that wage compression is indeed greatest in the first of these occupations, and least in the third.

In a subsequent paper, Alison Konrad and Jeffrey Pfeffer (1990) also examined pay distributions within work groups. They, too, found that wage compression was greatest in groups in which co-workers interacted most intensively. But where I argued that such a relationship was evidence of concerns about local status, Konrad and Pfeffer's account stressed the fairness model. With greater frequency of face-to-face interactions among co-workers, they argued, pay gaps would provoke increasing embarrassment on the part of the highest-paid workers, and increasing resentment on the part of those least well paid.

Thus the fact that pay compression appears to rise with the degree of interaction among co-workers may be taken as evidence in favor of both the local-status model and the fairness model. Unfortunately, it does nothing to help us choose between them.

A Preference for the Most Able Job Candidates

In an unpublished paper, David Romer (1992) observes that when firms are trying to fill positions, they almost invariably attempt to hire the most highly qualified candidates. This practice, he argues, is inconsistent with the view that firms pay workers their respective marginal products, for if that were the case, firms would be indifferent among applicants with differing levels of ability. Romer interprets the observed preference for the most able applicants as evidence for the fairness model of pay compression. Indeed, he goes so far as to say that other models of pay compression, including the local-status model, cannot explain this preference.

Romer is correct that a firm whose pay compression was the result of concerns about fairness would have every reason to prefer the most able job candidates. But I believe he is wrong to claim that the same preference cannot be explained by the local-status model. Consider, for example, Firm 1 in figure 6.2, in which the highest-paid worker is initially located at H and the lowest-paid worker at L. Suppose that, in accord with the local-status model, H and L and their co-workers are initially pleased with their chosen combinations of monetary wages and local status, and that Firm 1 initially earns zero economic profit. Now suppose Firm 1 hires a worker with productivity $M_D > M_H$ and compensates him according to the extension of its existing wage schedule. This new worker would become the highest paid worker in Firm 1 and would occupy the point labeled D, where he is paid a wage of W_D^1. If nothing else changed, Firm 1 would now be earning economic profits of $M_D - W_D^1$.

Of course, other things may change since D's presence also upsets the existing status ordering on which Firm 1's original wage structure was predicated. For one thing, H would no longer be the top-ranked worker, and might understandably feel that $M_H - W_H$ is too much to pay for a second-ranked position. He might then leave to join some other firm, or he might remain in Firm 1. If he stays, Firm 1's economic profits hold at $M_D - W_D^1$. If H leaves, Firm 1 earns economic profits of $(M_D - W_D^1) - (M_H - W_H) > 0$. Either way, Firm 1 ends up better off than before it hired D. The reason, of course, is that D is paying more than the market value of a top-ranked position, which he could have had at a wage of $W_D^2 > W_D^1$ had he joined Firm 2 instead of Firm 1.

Assuming that conditions apart from status orderings and wages in Firm 1 and Firm 2 are the same, this suggests that D simply must not have known about the possibility of working for Firm 2. Ignorance of this sort is surely common since it would hardly be rational for job seekers to be perfectly informed about all possible vacancies in the labor market.

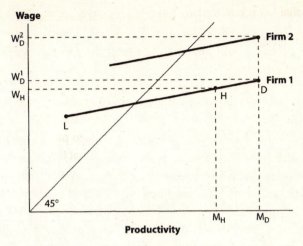

Figure 6.2 The Effect of Hiring a New Top Worker

As firms attempt to fill vacancies, they will naturally be delighted to hire highly qualified workers who may not be aware of more favorable opportunities elsewhere. So even if concerns about local status were the only factor that led to pay compression, firms would still have a clear motive to hire the most able job applicants under their prevailing wage structure. And thus, notwithstanding Romer's claim to the contrary, the near-universal preference for hiring the most qualified applicants provides no basis on which to discriminate between the local-status and fairness models.

Co-Worker Attitudes toward a More Productive Newcomer

The local-status model might seem inconsistent with the observation that co-workers are more likely to be pleased than displeased when their employer hires a conspicuously well-qualified person. This seems especially so in academia, where there is often a palpable air of good cheer when a department hires a star. But this reaction is perfectly consistent with the local-status model. As we saw in the previous section, when a well-qualified outsider joins a firm under an existing wage schedule that embodies compensating differentials for local status, there will always be at least as much surplus as before to divide among the incumbent employees. What is more, a well-qualified newcomer boosts the group's status vis-à-vis other groups, and this, too, must be counted as a benefit. Thus the observation that co-workers are pleased at the arrival of a highly qualified recruit should not lead us to favor the fairness model over the local-status model.

ARE THE TWO MODELS SIMPLY THE SAME?

In the discussion thus far, the predictions of both the fairness and local-status models have been essentially the same. When someone complains that a more productive colleague's higher pay is unfair, is he really just saying that he doesn't like being outdone? Perhaps concerns about fairness are in some fundamental way isomorphic to concerns about status.

To be sure, the two sets of concerns do appear to have important elements in common. For example, both concerns focus on the distribution of wages within the work group. Yet there remains an important distinction between concerns about fairness and concerns about status. Someone who cares primarily about status, for example, will tend to focus on a measure — such as his percentile ranking among his co-workers — that summarizes how he stands vis-à-vis others in the firm. In contrast, someone who cares primarily about fairness will focus on the amount of dispersion in the firm's wage distribution — as measured, say, by the variance or range of that distribution; she will be less concerned about what position she herself occupies in that distribution.

This distinction is undoubtedly an oversimplification, yet it highlights at least some of the similarities and differences of how the two concerns might translate into observable behavior. Consider again, for example, Guth, Schmittberger, and Schwarze's ultimatum bargaining game. We may view the two players, Proposer and Responder, as a local reference group in which each is concerned with the distribution not of wage income but of the surplus from the game. Do the local-status and fairness models make different predictions about Responder's reaction to a one-sided offer? Suppose Proposer has $100 to distribute and offers $10 to Responder, the remaining $90 to himself. If Responder refuses, he loses $10. But if he accepts, there is a distributional cost under both the fairness and local-status models. And if this cost is large enough, it may lead Responder to reject the offer. (Recall that when he rejects, each party gets zero, in which case there is no distributional cost in either model.)

As in the earlier cases we examined, then, the observation that one-sided offers are often rejected in the ultimatum bargaining game does not help us to discriminate between the two models. But as I will argue in the next section, status concerns do not always result in the same behaviors as fairness concerns.

The Disequilibrium Character of the Fairness Model

Consider the two firms whose wage schedules are shown in figure 6.3. Both schedules manifest the phenomenon to be explained, namely a more compressed distribution of wages than the corresponding distribution of productivity.

The pay distributions of both firms also fit the respective narratives of the local-status and fairness models. Consider, for example, the most productive worker in Firm 1, who is located at A. In terms of the local-status model, the high rank he enjoys comes at the expense of being paid less than his marginal product, the difference being distributed among his lesser-ranked co-workers. In terms of the fairness model, the worker at A enjoys the direct psychological benefits associated with the firm's equitable pay structure, plus any material benefits that may stem from high morale on the part of his co-workers. Because of the relatively small differences in pay among workers, he is not embarrassed about being the highest paid, nor do his less productive colleagues feel resentful about him.

So far, so good. But now the fairness model must confront this awkward question: Why shouldn't the individual located at A strictly prefer to change places with the least productive worker in Firm 2 (who is located at A' in figure 6.3)? By so doing, his wage would rise from W_A to $W_{A'}$ — a clear advantage under the assumed nature of his concerns — and since the wage structures of the two firms embody an equal degree of pay compression, there is no offsetting disadvantage along the fairness dimension.

The problem, in a nutshell, is that the fairness model of pay compression is not an equilibrium model. For, under that model, the top-ranked workers in any firm will always want to change places with the bottom-

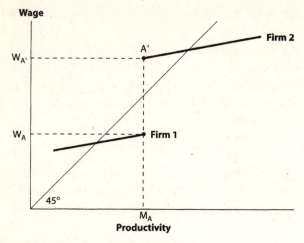

Figure 6.3 Choosing between the Two Models

ranked workers of firms with higher average productivity. The fairness model implies excess demand for bottom-ranked positions, excess supply of top-ranked positions.

Under the local-status model, by contrast, the worker at A has no motive to change places with the worker at A', for the value to him of the higher monetary wages would be smaller than the value of the loss in local status. Where the fairness model is a disequilibrium model of wage compression, the local-status model provides an equilibrium account of the same phenomenon.

Romer is the only author in the fairness literature whose model recognizes the significance of this distinction. He posits imperfect information and other frictions as the forces that might sustain what would otherwise be an unstable allocation. In effect, the top-ranked workers do not move either because they do not know about the more attractive alternatives, or because they have acquired commitments that make it too costly to move.

Who could deny that information about alternative job openings is invariably far from perfect? Or that local commitments often make it unattractive to leave one job for another? Yet despite the clear importance of these frictions, we must question whether they could systematically prevent the kinds of welfare-improving moves predicted by the fairness model. The strength of local commitments, for example, will vary systematically by industry and location. Firm-specific human capital, a source of local commitment in some industries, is relatively unimportant in many others. In large labor markets, there may be many employers in a given industry, and moving from one to another need not entail geographical relocation or even a change of school districts. Nor is it likely that workers in a given area will be uninformed about wage scales at competing employers in the same area. If concerns about fairness were the only force behind wage compression, these cases would provide an arbitrage opportunity for anyone willing to bid for the top-ranked workers from firms in a given labor market. An entrepreneur could offer a wage structure with higher wages than in existing firms and with equally low variance, and at the same time earn substantial economic profits. And yet substantial wage compression remains the rule, even where labor-market frictions appear minimal.

Until we see evidence for the existence of frictions strong enough to prevent this from happening, we must be skeptical that concerns about fairness are by themselves sufficient to explain pay compression. Concerns about local status, by contrast, can sustain pay compression even in perfectly frictionless labor markets.

CONCLUDING REMARKS

There is an oft-told story of a boy who found two ripe apples as he was walking home from school with a friend. He kept the larger one for himself and gave the smaller one to his friend. The friend's obvious look of distress led the first boy to inquire what was the matter.

"It wasn't fair to keep the larger one for yourself," the friend replied.

"What would you have done?" the first boy asked.

"I'd have given you the larger one and kept the smaller one for myself," said the friend. To which the first boy responded,

"Well, we each got what you wanted, so what are you complaining about?"

Concerns about status and fairness are multidimensional and complex. Outcomes are important, but the process by which the outcomes are reached also matters. To model concerns about status and fairness as concerns about pay rank and variance is to ignore process concerns completely, and may indeed miss much about our concerns about outcomes. Surely many people care, for example, not just about where they rank in the local pay distribution, but also about how far they are from the highest-paid worker, from the median worker, and so on. Existing work simply fails to capture these distinctions.

But even the primitive state of current research allows us to say something. There is abundant evidence that people care about both fairness and local status. On the basis of either of these concerns — no matter how clumsily specified — it follows logically that workers would abandon a firm in which pay was exactly equal to marginal productivity to join an alternative firm with slightly smaller pay differences among workers. The simple logic of supply and demand suggests that a stable equilibrium with pay compression is possible only in the presence of concerns about local status. Our ability to make more detailed statements about how concerns about both fairness and local status affect behavior will depend in large part on our ability to capture these concerns in formal theoretical models, and then test their implications empirically.

7

Motivation, Cognition, and Charitable Giving

IN A MONTY PYTHON SKIT, John Cleese plays a banker who is asked to donate a pound to a local orphanage. His first reaction is that the solicitor must be proposing an investment opportunity, or possibly a tax dodge. Neither, the solicitor tells him, at which point Cleese is nonplused.

> CLEESE: No? Well, I'm awfully sorry I don't understand. Can you just explain exactly what you want.
>
> SOLICITOR: Well, I want you to give me a pound, and then I go away and give it to the orphans.
>
> CLEESE: Yes?
>
> SOLICITOR: Well, that's it.
>
> CLEESE: No, no, no, I don't follow this at all, I mean, I don't want to seem stupid but it looks to me as though I'm a pound down on the whole deal.
>
> SOLICITOR: Well, yes you are.
>
> CLEESE: I am! Well, what is my incentive to give you the pound?
>
> SOLICITOR: Well, the incentive is — to make the orphans happy.
>
> CLEESE: (genuinely puzzled) Happy? . . . You're quite sure you've got this right?
>
> (Chapman 1989, pp. 93–94)

Cleese nicely epitomizes the *homo economicus* stereotype who populates the self-interest models that increasingly dominate theoretical work in the social sciences. In these models, moral sentiments play no role. *Homo economicus* does not vote in presidential elections; he does not recycle; he does not leave tips when dining on the road; he pours unwanted pesticides down his basement drain; and, most certainly, he does not make anonymous donations to private charities.

Yet despite the ascendancy of narrow self-interest models, most of us are amused by Cleese's portrayal of the selfish banker. And notwithstanding the predictions of these models, we give large sums to private charities. In 1992 alone, for example, Americans gave more than $250 billion, an average of more than $2000 per family (Freeman 1993), a figure that includes an estimate of the value of time spent in volunteer activities.

The dominant behavioral models in the social sciences view people not only as self-interested, but also as rational. Although these models freely acknowledge that people often lack the information needed to make perfect decisions, the assumption is that people act rationally on the basis of whatever information they do have. Yet here, too, examples to the contrary abound.

Psychologists Amos Tversky and Daniel Kahneman (1981), for instance, told one group of experimental subjects to imagine that, having earlier purchased tickets for $10, they arrive at the theater to discover they have lost them. They told members of a second group to picture themselves arriving just before the performance to buy their tickets when they find that they have each lost $10 from their wallets. People in both groups were then asked whether they would continue with their plans to attend the performance. If people are rational, the distribution of answers should be the same for both groups, since in each case the relevant change is that the decision maker is $10 poorer than before. And yet, in repeated trials, most people in the lost-ticket group said they would not attend the performance, while an overwhelming majority— 88 percent—in the lost-bill group said they would.

In this chapter, I will argue that the narrow rational actor model provides a poor basis for thinking about the behavior of charitable organizations and the people who support them. I will begin by noting that, even in the most bitterly competitive environments, we should expect not just the narrowly selfish human motives emphasized in modern social science, but also motives of a more genuinely altruistic sort. I will suggest that although charities can hope to win support from both altruistic and selfish persons, the most effective strategies for appealing to these two types of donors will often be very different from one another. Finally, I will examine the implications of recent research in cognitive psychology for charitable giving.

HUMAN MOTIVATION IN COMPETITIVE ENVIRONMENTS

To study charitable giving, or indeed any other human behavior, we must begin with basic assumptions about human motivation. The dominant model in the contemporary social sciences is the self-interest model of rational choice, which assumes that people have essentially selfish goals and pursue them efficiently.

Cynical though it may appear, this model has yielded important insights. It tells us why people buy more fuel-efficient cars in the wake of rising gasoline prices; why people are more likely to recycle when garbage collection is billed by the container; why speeding is less common in states with high traffic fines; and so on.

Yet, as noted in preceding chapters, many other behaviors do not fit the me-first caricature. The irony, as we have seen, is that many noble human behaviors not only survive the ruthless pressures of the material world, but are nurtured by them, as well. If this claim seems self-contradictory, it is no more so than the fact that someone who deliberately tries to be "more spontaneous" is destined to fail. In the course of social and economic interaction, we confront many problems in which the conscious, direct pursuit of self-interest is self-defeating.

The ecological framework described in chapter 1 provides theoretical underpinning for a remarkably commonsensical portrait of human nature. It tells us that people are driven by a combination of selfish and altruistic motives, just as experience seems to suggest. Although the mix of motives is highly variable across individuals, it is rare to see individuals who are driven exclusively by purely selfish or purely altruistic motives. It is instructive, for example, that the investment banker portrayed by John Cleese is such a comic figure.

In the eighteenth and nineteenth centuries, expansive views about human nature almost invariably characterized writings about human behavior. Contemporary social scientists, by contrast, increasingly ignore all but selfish motives. To their credit, however, modern scholars have developed much more carefully elaborated theories about how selfish motives translate into behavior in different domains. Our challenge here is to discover how these theories play out under a broader conception of human motivation.

MOTIVES FOR GIVING

Once we acknowledge that people are driven in part by altruistic motives, we can construct a simple, if uninteresting, theory of charitable giving. People donate because they *like* to donate, or at least feel it their duty to do so. There are several reasons people might take pleasure in giving. They might like the fact that their gifts will be put to specific uses of which they strongly approve. Many of those who donate to CARE's efforts on behalf of sub-Saharan famine victims fall into this category.

In other cases, altruistic giving need not signal approval of the specific disposition of the donated funds. Many donors, for example, derive satisfaction from providing extra resources to the impoverished, even though they may not approve of the specific uses to which those resources are put.

Note, however, that one can give to a cause one cares strongly about even in the absence of altruistic motives. The entire community may benefit from having a safe water supply, yet there may be only a single individual with sufficient resources to build a treatment facility. If that person has a sufficiently strong personal interest in safe water, it may pay for her to build the facility on her own. And once developed, it may cost nothing extra to make safe water available to others.

But cases like this are surely rare. They should not be confused with much more common instances of donors who stand to benefit if the charitable organization's mission is carried out successfully. Suppose, for example, that generous relief for the poor would eliminate crime in the streets. Might not a person's gift to, say, The Salvation Army, then be rationalized by a narrowly selfish desire not to be victimized by street crime? Likewise, could not a gift to the Public Broadcasting System be viewed as a self-interested attempt to keep the NewsHour on the air? Except in unusual cases, the answer seems to be no. The problem is that the typical individual gift is far too small to affect the outcome in question. Any one person's risk of being a street-crime victim is virtually unaffected by even a generous gift to The Salvation Army. Similarly, the status of the NewsHour is, for all practical purposes, independent of any one person's gift. To explain such gifts, we must invoke some sort of altruistic motive (on this point, see Andreoni [1986]).

There are also cases in which donors benefit, even in narrowly material terms, by making gifts to charities about whose work they care not at all. For example, some donors may be subject to regulation in their business dealings, and being known as community benefactors may entitle them to more favorable treatment in the political arena. More generally, people may give because enhanced status is of value for its own sake, quite apart from any material benefits it may yield. Even in these cases, however, the altruistic concerns of the population at large will shape charitable giving. After all, a gift to a cause that few people favor will do little to enhance the donor's reputation.

A related selfish motive for giving is the desire to gain access to favored social networks. As with higher status, enhanced social contacts may be a source of pleasure in their own right. But as sociologists are quick to emphasize, they also have an important instrumental character. The allocation of jobs and other important resources, for example, are often decisively influenced by membership in social networks (Granovetter 1972, 1985; Podolny 1993).

That many gifts are consistent with self-interested motives is further underscored by the observation that the gifts of many donors come not at the expense of personal consumption but of leaving a smaller estate at their time of death. This is certainly true of the extremely wealthy, but is true of many others, as well. In such cases, a gift involves no sacrifice in the donor's current or future living standards, yet may benefit the donor in any of the ways mentioned earlier.

To recapitulate briefly, my aim in this section has been to make clear that we may speak intelligibly of altruistic motives even within the bitterly competitive materialistic framework popular in the modern social sciences. This is not to deny, of course, the importance of selfish motives, which co-mingle with altruistic motives in most people. My claim is that any theory of charitable giving based exclusively on one type of motive or the other will inevitably fail to capture an essential aspect of reality.

Motivation is not the only respect in which conventional models of rational choice paint a misleading picture of human behavior. These models also assume that people are efficient in pursuit of their goals. But as the following brief review of recent findings in cognitive psychology will make clear, there are systematic exceptions even to this more limited claim.

DEPARTURES FROM RATIONAL CHOICE

The Asymmetric Value Function

The rational choice model says that people should evaluate events, or collections of events, in terms of their overall effect on total wealth. Suppose you get an unexpected gift of $100 and then you return from vacation to find an $80 invoice from the city for the repair of a broken water line on your property. According to the rational choice model, you should regard the occurrence of these two events as a good thing, because their net effect is a $20 increase in your total wealth.

Amos Tversky and Daniel Kahneman (1981) argue, however, that people often seem to weigh each event separately, and attach considerably less importance to the gain than to the loss—so much less that many people actually refuse to accept pairs of events that would increase their overall wealth. They propose that people evaluate alternatives not with the conventional utility function of rational choice theory, but instead with a value function defined over *changes* in wealth. One important property of this value function is that it is much steeper in losses than in gains. In figure 7.1, for example, note how it assigns a much larger value, in absolute terms, to a loss of $80 than to a gain of $100. Note also that the value function is concave in gains and convex in losses. This means that the psychological impact of incremental gains or losses diminishes as the gains or losses become larger.

According to Tversky and Kahneman, it is very common for people to evaluate each item of a collection of events separately, then make decisions on the basis of the sum of the separate values. In this example, $V(100)$ is much smaller, in absolute terms, than $V(-80)$. Because the algebraic sum of the two is less than zero, anyone who employs this decision mechanism will refuse this pair of opportunities even though their net effect is to increase total wealth by $20.

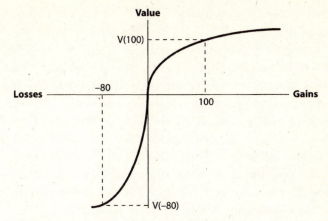

Figure 7.1 The Tversky-Kahneman Value Function

There are really two important features of the Tversky and Kahneman value function. One is that people treat gains and losses asymmetrically, giving the latter much heavier weight in their decisions than the former. The second is that people evaluate events first, then add the separate values together. The first of these features does not necessarily imply irrational behavior. There is nothing inconsistent, after all, about feeling that a loss causes more pain relative to the happiness caused by a gain of the same magnitude. What *does* often appear irrational is the second step — treating each event separately, rather than considering their combined effect.

This is essentially a question about how to frame events. If someone pointed out to a person that the net effect of two events A and B was to increase her wealth by $20 she would probably quickly agree to allow the events to happen. Framed as an entity, they are obviously an improvement over the status quo. The problem is that, in actual decisions, it may seem more natural to frame the events separately. And, as we will see, this tendency has implications for charitable giving.

Sunk Costs

Another basic tenet of rational choice theory is that sunk costs should be ignored in decisions. Contrary to this claim, sunk costs often appear to weigh quite heavily. Economist Richard Thaler (1980) offers the following example: Suppose you have just paid $40 for tickets to a basketball game to be played tonight in an arena sixty miles north of your home. Suddenly it starts snowing heavily and the roads north, while passable, are difficult. Do you still go to the game? Would your answer have been different if, instead of having bought the tickets, you had received them for free? Thaler finds that most people who bought the tickets would go, whereas most of those who were given them say they would stay home. According to the rational choice model, of course, the decision should be the same in either case. If your expected pleasure of seeing the game exceeds the expected hassle of the drive, you should go; otherwise stay home. Neither element in this cost-benefit calculation should depend on how you obtained the tickets.

Out-of-Pocket Costs vs. Opportunity Costs

Thaler suggests that our tendency not to ignore sunk costs may be given a simple interpretation in terms of the Tversky and Kahneman value function (1980). Tickets to the 2002 Super Bowl sold for $350 through official channels, but in the open market went for prices as high as $6000. Thousands of fans used their $350 tickets to attend the game, thus passing up the opportunity to sell them for $6000. Very few of these fans, however, would have spent $6000 to buy a ticket for the game. Thaler suggests that people code the $350 expense as a loss, but the $6000 opportunity cost as a forgone gain.

Hedonic Framing

Tversky and Kahneman's value function suggests specific ways that sellers, gift givers, and others might frame their offerings to enhance their appeal. Thaler (1985) mentions several specific strategies.

SEGREGATE GAINS. Because the value function is concave in gains, a higher total value results when we decompose a large gain into two (or more) smaller ones. Thus, for example, figure 7.2 shows that a gain of one hundred creates more total value if decomposed into two separate gains of sixty and forty. The moral here, as Thaler puts it, is "Don't wrap all the Christmas presents in a single box."

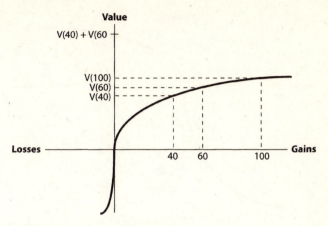

Figure 7.2 The Benefit of Segregating Gains

COMBINE LOSSES. The convexity of the value function in the loss domain implies that two separate losses will appear less painful if they are
combined into a single, larger loss. As shown in figure 7.3, for example,
separate losses of twenty and thirty have a combined value that is larger,
in absolute terms, than the value of a loss of fifty.

SEGREGATE SMALL GAINS FROM LARGE LOSSES. A sample of subjects
was asked which of these persons is more upset: A, whose car sustains
$200 damage in the parking lot the same day he wins $25 in the office
football pool; or B, whose car sustains $175 damage in the parking lot?
72 percent responded that B would be more upset, 22 percent picked A,
and 6 percent said they would be equally upset. The rational choice
model predicts they would be equally upset, because they suffer exactly
the same reduction in their wealth. The Tversky and Kahneman value
function, by contrast, predicts that B would be more upset, which ac-
cords with most people's responses. Thaler calls the segregation of a
small gain from a big loss the "silver lining effect," and argues that it
may help explain why so many merchants offer cash rebates on their
products. ("Buy a new Dodge before October 1 and get $1,200 cash
back!") Viewed in the context of the rational choice model, this practice
seems to be dominated by the simple alternative of reducing the price of

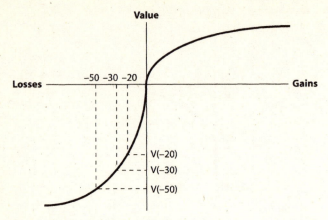

Figure 7.3 The Benefit of Combining Losses

the product, which would lower the total amount of sales tax the buyer pays.

The Psychophysics of Perception

There is yet another pattern to the way we perceive and process information that differs from the predictions of the rational choice model. It derives from the so-called Weber-Fechner law of psychophysics. Weber and Fechner set out to discover how large the change in a stimulus had to be before we could perceive the difference in intensity. Most people, for example, are unable to distinguish a 100-watt light bulb from a 100.5-watt light bulb. But how large does the difference in brightness have to be before people can reliably identify it? Weber and Fechner found that the minimally perceptible difference is roughly proportional to the original intensity of the stimulus. Thus the more intense the stimulus is, the larger the difference has to be, in absolute terms, before we can tell the difference.

The Weber-Fechner law seems to be at work when people decide whether price differences are worth worrying about. Suppose, for example, you are about to buy a clock radio in a store for $25 when a friend informs you that the same radio is selling for only $20 in another store only 10 minutes away. Do you go to the other store? Would your answer have been different if you had been about to buy a television for $500 and your friend told you the same set was available at the other store for only $495? Most people answer yes to the first question, no to the second.

In the rational choice model, it is inconsistent to answer differently for the two cases. A rational person will travel to the other store if and only if the benefits of doing so exceed the costs. The benefit is $5 in both cases. The cost is also the same for each trip, whether it is to buy a radio or a television. If it makes sense to go in one case, it also makes sense in the other.

Earlier proponents of the rational choice model were under no illusions that people were flawless decision makers. But early research on decision making under incomplete information seemed to suggest that any departures of behavior from fully informed rational choices were essentially random. By contrast, more recent research in this area suggests that the rules of thumb people use, although adaptive in many contexts, often give rise to systematic departures from rational choice. What is more, many errors occur predictably in contexts where decision makers have all the relevant information at hand.

SOME IMPLICATIONS FOR FUNDRAISERS

In this section, I will consider how the preceding discussion of motivation and cognition might be put to use by the managers of charitable organizations.

The Strategic Problem of Appealing to Multiple Motives

Earlier we saw that charitable organizations can hope to appeal even to potential donors who are motivated primarily by narrow self-interest. And there has never been any mystery about how charitable organizations might appeal to donors with altruistic motives. Once we recognize the plurality of motives for giving, however, any given charitable organization's task becomes more complex. Indeed, it may seem natural to question whether a single charity can hope to appeal simultaneously to both altruistic and selfish motives.

Yet consider the difficulty of a charity that attempted to appeal only to donors with selfish motives. As noted, charitable organizations have much to offer such persons, both in terms of business and regulatory contacts and heightened status and respect in the community. The fundamental problem is that the community is more likely to admire donors whose gifts are motivated by altruism than by self-interest. Of course, outsiders have little way of knowing what any individual donor's motives might be. But if a charity openly appealed to selfish motives, and managed in the process to attract primarily selfish donors, it would eventually be colored by a community perception to that effect. Such a charity would thus be ill positioned to confer status upon its donors, and hence less able to attract the kinds of donors with whom selfish donors might wish to associate. These considerations suggest that if a charity is to appeal to selfish motives, it must do so indirectly.

There is a parallel difficulty, however, that confronts any charity that ignores the self-interested motives of potential donors. Most donors, even those with strongly altruistic concerns, have narrowly self-interested goals as well. Consider a charity that determinedly resists any opportunity to facilitate its donors' pursuit of selfish objectives. It collects their donations for an unquestionably worthy cause, but resists any step that might create advantages for them in the community. It does not publicly recognize major gifts, it does not hold social events, and so on. Charitable giving is an intensely competitive industry. Support for many worthy causes is organized by charitable groups that afford donors public recognition for large gifts, chances to mingle socially, and so on. Facing competitive pressures from charities organized along these broader lines, it would be difficult for a charity to survive if it refused to acknowledge, and attempt to serve, its donors' self-interested motives.

Note the parallels between the forces that govern the evolution of different types of motives in human populations and those that govern the evolution of different types of charitable organizations. In both cases it appears that populations consisting only of pure types are unlikely to be evolutionarily stable. In human populations consisting only of trustworthy persons, the level of vigilance will be low, which in turn will enable cheaters to make inroads. Likewise, in an environment in which all charitable organizations ignored the self-interested motives of their donors, there would be opportunities for organizations that took these motives into account.

At the other end of the scale, human populations in which cheaters predominate give rise to a climate of vigilance that fosters the growth of cooperative motives. The analog in the organizational context is that an environment consisting of charitable organizations that catered only to the selfish motives of donors would foster the growth of new organizations that broadened their appeal to include altruistic motives.

In sum, it appears that ecological forces will give rise to human populations in which most people pursue a mix of selfish and altruistic motives, and a population of charitable organizations in which most groups attempt to appeal simultaneously to both types of motives. This characterization of charitable organizations and their donors has numerous specific implications for how these organizations might appeal most effectively for support.

The Central Role of the Cause Itself

Perhaps the most important message is that despite the importance of self-interested motives for most donors, a charitable organization's appeal for support must focus primarily on the worthiness of its cause. A campaign that begins with a fundamentally worthy cause at its core then has many opportunities to enhance its appeal by providing donors with opportunities to advance a variety of self-interested goals. But one that lacks a worthy cause is, for the reasons discussed earlier, almost certain to fail.

The Role of Affect

Many gifts are motivated not by rational deliberations about self-interest but rather by moral sentiments like sympathy and guilt. The most effective appeal in these cases will thus focus on triggering the relevant emotions. That this principle is well understood by many charitable organizations is evident from specific strategies for personalizing both the cause and the direct connection between organization and donor. Let us briefly consider these in turn.

STATISTICAL VERSUS IDENTIFIED LIVES. Thomas Schelling (1984) cites the example of a community that is willing to spend several million dollars to rescue a child trapped in an abandoned mine shaft, yet is unwilling to spend half a million dollars on an emergency coronary care ambulance that will save an average of five lives per year. The explanation is not that the community values the lives of trapped children much more in the abstract than it does the lives of potential heart attack victims. On the contrary, the community might very well be willing to spend even less per expected life saved on measures to prevent accidents in mines than on measures to save heart attack victims. Rather, the critical difference is that the child trapped in the mine is a known individual while the potential beneficiaries of the coronary care units are merely statistics. We see the child's grieving parents, we imagine ourselves in their position, we contemplate our sense of remorse if we fail to intervene. An identified life is vivid — it engages our emotions fully. Of course, we know in the abstract that future coronary victims will also be real people with grieving relatives. But the power of these imagined victims to engage our sympathies is much more limited. And hence the difference in our willingness to expend resources in the two situations.

Many charitable organizations appear to have grasped the importance of tying their cause to the plight of specific identified individuals. The March of Dimes, for example, has its poster child, and the Jerry Lewis telethons bring the beneficiaries into our living rooms. CARE knows that a photograph of a starving child will summon many more donations than an abstract appeal to end world hunger.

PERSONAL SOLICITATION. Richard Freeman (1993) has found that, holding the worthiness of the cause constant, people are much more likely to make charitable donations when they are asked than when they are not. People understandably feel that there are many more causes that deserve support than they can possibly support themselves. One could of course apportion one's limited support on the basis of an abstract assessment of the relative merits of the various causes. But it is hardly surprising that a given cause is more likely to make a donor's short list if it appeals to her directly. Most people are strongly motivated to win the approval of other people — friends in particular, and, to a lesser degree, even strangers. Failure to donate to an organization that doesn't ask courts no risk of face-to-face disapproval. When a friend requests a donation for a worthy cause, by contrast, both the abstract desire to support the cause and the more concrete motivation to please the friend work in tandem. Most charities are aware of this, of course, and rely on volunteer networks to solicit friends.

OPPORTUNITIES FOR ANONYMITY. Although many, perhaps even most, donors find public recognition gratifying, there are at least some with a strong preference to remain out of the limelight. This group will include some whose motive is to avoid being solicited by charities they have no wish to support. But it will also include some whose pleasure in giving is enhanced by the fact that it was in no way motivated by the hope to win others' approval. Still others may wish to give anonymously in the secret hope that their identities will somehow leak out, thereby placing them in the admirable, if paradoxical, position of being known as generous anonymous givers. Attempts to accommodate such donors are fraught with practical difficulties, although we may suspect that in equilibrium there will inevitably be organizations that are willing discreetly to leak the identities of anonymous donors.

That there exist donors who prefer anonymity does not mean that organizations should call public attention to the fact that they offer opportunities for anonymous giving. Public announcements to that effect may create the impression that donations that receive public recognition are somehow less praiseworthy. Even if this is true, it is no reason to discourage donors who seek public approval. And in any event, those who really want to donate anonymously hardly need to be made aware of that possibility through public pronouncements. A charity need only recognize that some such donors exist, and to make every effort to maintain confidentiality if that is the donor's desire.

MATCHING GRANTS. Many charitable organizations have discovered the efficacy of matching grants — contingent donations under which a benefactor pledges to match others' gifts up to some specified amount. From the perspectives both of the initiator of a matching grant offer and of those who respond to it, this practice creates additional leverage. And if the ceiling of the benefactor's grant is not reached, or if the benefactor would not have given as much on other terms, the format does indeed increase total giving. Given that matching grants have positive effects and are virtually costless to administer, the puzzle is that they are not used even more widely. Even someone contemplating a $100 gift to her local radio station, for example, could achieve more impact by making her gift a matching grant. Yet most small donations are not in the form of matching grants.

MARKETING STATUS. People acquire status in a variety of ways, almost all of which involve being compared favorably with other persons. Status acquisition thus has a zero-sum character. Actions or behaviors that enhance one actor's status involve reductions in status for others. When we frame the issue in these stark terms, it seems natural to wonder whether charitable organizations ought to act as agents in their donors' quest for status.

A moment's reflection about alternatives, however, suggests that this is an attractive role, indeed. After all, the quest for status would continue unabated even if charities stood completely aloof from it; and many of the alternative means of pursuing social status are distinctly less attractive than charitable giving. For example, many people display their wealth by conspicuous consumption. From a social perspective, such behavior is a wasteful alternative to the display of wealth by charitable giving (Frank 1985; Glazer and Konrad 1992).

If a charitable organization wants to facilitate potential donors' quest for status, what can it do? One valuable service is to create opportunities for their leading donors to mingle with one another, as in fact many charitable and other nonprofit institutions routinely do. Universities, for example, often appoint, and convene regular meetings of, advisory councils that include their leading benefactors. The "charity ball" is another time-honored institution in this tradition. Still another device is to recognize donors by attaching their names to facilities, positions, or projects, as when a university creates an endowed professorship in a donor's name.

All these activities confront the organization with the strategic calculation of how to distribute recognition and opportunities for association in the way that maximizes total value. To take an illustrative case, consider a university's decision about how many endowed professorships to create. The law of demand states that the lower the price of a good or service, the more units of it the public will wish to buy. Put slightly differently, it says that the more units of a good or service people already have, the less they will be willing to pay for an additional unit. This proposition will hold doubly for a "good" like public recognition, for as an institution attempts to distribute ever more recognition to its donors, its power to confer effective recognition on any of them diminishes sharply.

If the university charges each donor the same price for the right to endow a chair, and its goal is to maximize its total revenues from donors, at what level should it set the price? An extremely high price (say, $20 million per chair) would produce only limited revenue, since few donors would be willing to endow a chair at that price. If the demand curve for chairs were roughly linear, the typical pattern would be for price cuts from that initial high level to stimulate enough additional sales to more than offset the lost revenue per chair. Beyond some point, however, further price reductions typically become counterproductive. The revenue gained from additional sales no longer is sufficient to compensate for the loss suffered by selling each chair at a lower price.

Suppose that the revenue-maximizing price for an endowed chair turns out to be $3 million (roughly the current price for such chairs at Ivy League schools). Selling all chairs at that single price is inefficient from the perspective of both the university and its donors. There is no physical cost when a standard faculty position is transformed into an endowed position, and yet there are many potential donors who cannot or will not endow a chair at $3 million even though they would be happy to donate $1 million or even $2 million for the privilege. Failure to include these donors makes both them and the university worse off.

Another source of inefficiency occurs at the other end of the donor spectrum. There are many donors who would have been willing to pay much more than $3 million for the privilege of endowing a chair, and at least some would actually have preferred that the group of people whose names are attached to chaired professorships be smaller, and hence more elite.

From the perspective of professors, as well, the practice of selling all chairs for the same price is inefficient. Among the group of professors not holding endowed chairs, for instance, there are many who feel themselves worthy, and indeed many who genuinely are worthy, of holding such positions. And among the most distinguished of those currently holding endowed chairs, there will be some who wish the number of chairs was considerably smaller than the current level.

By tinkering slightly with its endowed-chair pricing policy, the university can mitigate many of these inefficiencies. Suppose, for example, that in addition to the standard endowed chair it currently offers, it adds a premium category with a title something like "distinguished university professorship." Chairs in both categories would bear the names of their respective donors, as now, but the distinguished professorship would sell for a premium price, say, $5 million, while the ordinary endowed professorship might sell for $2 million. With suitably chosen prices for the different types of chairs, the university could increase the total revenue from the sale of endowed chairs. What is more, it could also increase the total surplus reaped by participating donors (defined as the sum over all donors of the difference between the largest amount each donor would have been willing to pay and the amount he or she actually does pay).

The number of categories of course need not be limited to two, and in general the more finely the market can be partitioned, the smaller the unexploited surplus will be. Nor need the process be limited to the endowment of chairs. At the higher end, it can include endowed buildings, and even colleges. At the lower end it can include relatively modest scholarship or research endowments. Some institutions even allow donors to purchase named seats in auditoriums.

Issues similar to those that arise in connection with the marketing of endowed professorships, programs, and facilities are encountered in a host of other contexts. Universities elect boards of trustees, whose positions they reserve for their most influential and generous supporters. Often they also maintain much larger advisory councils, and here membership is more inclusive. Many other charities maintain several tiers of advisory boards, and also sponsor larger gatherings of supporters, such as annual social events. In all of these cases, the interests of donors and beneficiaries alike can be advanced by careful attention to the partitioning of the relevant markets.

Framing Manipulations

The recent work in cognitive psychology summarized earlier suggests a variety of possible ways in which a charity might frame its appeal for greatest effectiveness.

IN-KIND CONTRIBUTIONS. Richard Thaler (1980) describes the incongruous example of the man who would not mow his neighbor's lawn for $20, yet mows his own lawn even though his neighbor's son would be willing to do it for only $8. The explanation, Thaler argues, is that people mentally code out-of-pocket expenses (here, the $8) as losses, but code opportunity costs (here, the $20 not earned by mowing the neighbor's lawn) as forgone gains. The asymmetry between gains and losses discussed earlier lies behind the man's seemingly inconsistent decision.

The knowledge that forgone gains are psychologically less painful than out-of-pocket expenses suggests that a charitable organization may often be able to increase its support by appealing for donations in kind rather than in cash. Many charities, for example, sponsor benefit concerts in which services are donated not only by the featured musicians, but also by a constellation of other, much less visible support personnel.

The same principle may help explain why the parents of children attending expensive private schools often spend harried Friday evenings preparing items for the school's semi-annual bake sale. Since most of these parents are highly paid professionals whose time is both scarce and valuable, it might seem more sensible for them simply to make additional cash contributions to their children's schools. The irony is that if out-of-pocket costs are accorded greater weight than opportunity costs, the bake sale may nonetheless be the more effective vehicle. Of course, bake sales and other in-kind contributions also promote social interaction, which may itself be of value to the donor.

"FREE" GIFTS TO DONORS. Many charitable organizations, among them public radio and television stations, offer contributors free gifts in return for their cash donations. This practice may seem puzzling at first glance, but on closer scrutiny it appears to make sense for at least several reasons. First, there is the silver lining effect, which says that the overall disutility of a loss will be significantly reduced if it can be framed as a package that includes a small gain. Here the cash contribution is the loss and the token gift the small gain.

Gifts to donors might also be attractive because the gifts themselves can often be obtained as gifts from their manufacturers, whose generosity is enhanced by the perception that forgone gains are coded as less pain-ful than out-of-pocket costs. Even without that perception, promotional gifts can generally be obtained at wholesale prices, whereas their value to donors is likely to be coded at the much higher retail prices. Another attractive feature of gifts is that they often bear the charity's logo, thereby calling favorable attention to a donor.

SELLING DISCOUNT COUPONS. In the private sector, retail merchants often band together to sell books of discount coupons, which entitle bearers to reduced prices on various goods and services. This device is attractive in part because it enables sellers to target discount prices at those buyers for whom lower prices are most likely to affect purchase decisions. The reasoning here is that buyers for whom price matters little are unlikely to go to the trouble of buying, storing for future use, and then redeeming discount coupons. Another attractive feature is that the coupon books, like many other promotional devices, are a useful way to introduce new buyers to products. Offering a deep discount is good busi-ness if the buyer turns out to like the product and becomes a regular customer. Finally, the discount coupon booklets may be attractive be-cause they encourage buyers to go to a particular retail district, where their trip to buy from one merchant may result in additional purchases from other merchants.

An interesting feature of discount coupon booklets is that, having bought one, people apparently feel duty-bound to use it, at least for a while. Standard economic theory suggests that, once bought, the pur-chase price of a coupon booklet is a sunk cost, and hence the likelihood of using particular coupons in it ought to depend only on how the dis-counted prices compare with how much value a consumer assigns to the various products. As with many other sunk costs, however, there is evi-dence that buyers do not ignore the sunk cost of these booklets. Often they buy products that as non-coupon-book purchasers they would not have bought even at similarly deep discounts.

Ironically, a different pattern holds when discount coupon booklets are sold not by merchants but by charitable organizations. Here, people seem to ignore the sunk cost of their booklets, just as traditional eco-nomic theory predicts (Nye 1993). People seem to encode the price of the booklets as a charitable donation, not as a sunk cost they need to justify by subsequent purchase behavior. As a result, it may be possible that when the proceeds from the sale of discount booklets accrue to charitable organizations, merchants may be able to offer even deeper discounts than before, and this in turn should raise the price that consumers are willing to pay for the booklets.

EARMARKING. The free-rider hypothesis of traditional rational choice models is predicated on the notion that any single donor's gift constitutes such a small proportion of a charity's overall budget that it cannot appreciably alter the extent to which the charity achieves its mission. If the charity will succeed or fail independently of your own contribution to it, the argument goes, then why make the personal sacrifice?

The Weber-Fechner law discussed earlier suggests a psychological mechanism whereby charitable organizations might reduce the attractiveness of free-riding. What an organization wants to prevent, specifically, is having the individual view her donation as a proportion of its overall budget. To this end, it can offer donors the opportunity to earmark their contributions for specific activities on a much smaller scale. Several decades ago, for example, I was a volunteer fund raiser in a political campaign and was surprised to discover that the fee for thirty-second radio commercials on local stations was only $10. We then framed our call for contributions as a request to fund individual radio spots ("Your gift of $100 will put 10 more George-Brown-for-Senate commercials on the air"), and donations increased substantially.

There is indirect evidence that giving donors a choice between funding any of several different specific activities may also enhance contributions. Gilovich (1991), for example, found that sales of state lottery tickets increase dramatically when consumers are given the opportunity to pick their own winning number, rather than having it assigned by a random number generator.

CONCLUDING REMARKS

In recent decades, the self-interest model of rational choice has become increasingly influential in the social and behavioral sciences. I have argued that this model provides an impoverished framework for thinking about the behavior of both charitable organizations and their donors.

The standard model is flawed not only in its characterization of human motives, but also in its portrayal of the efficacy with which people pursue these motives. Drawing on signaling and game theory in an evolutionary framework, I have described a broader portfolio of human motives, one that includes concerns not only about the well-being of others, but also about status in various social hierarchies. I have also described recent work in cognitive psychology that suggests that people often pursue their goals inefficiently, and that the errors they make are often systematic rather than random. Finally, I have tried to show how the insights of this recent work help us achieve a clearer understanding of what charitable organizations and their supporters are up to.

Part III

Forging Better Outcomes

8

Social Norms as Positional Arms-Control Agreements

THE TERM "positional arms race" refers to an escalating pattern of mutually offsetting investments undertaken by rivals whose rewards depend
on relative performance. Such arms races are abundant in social and
economic interaction — advertising wars, anabolic steroid consumption,
cram courses for the SATs, social and professional wardrobe expendi-
tures, even cosmetic surgery.

A variety of formal mechanisms — such as random drug testing of athletes and chronological age mandates for kindergarten students — have
been used to control positional arms races. In this chapter, I explore how
less formal mechanisms such as social norms and moral suasion have
served a similar function. Examples include social ostracism of "nerds"
by students; norms favoring modest standards of consumption; and implicit agreements among news organizations not to dwell on sensational
or lurid news stories.

POSITIONAL ARMS RACES

Economic and social life is replete with situations in which people's
rewards depend not only on their absolute performance, but also on how
well they perform relative to immediate rivals. Thus, the times posted by
swimmer Mark Spitz earned him seven gold medals in the 1976 Olympic Games, but would not even have qualified him for the most recent
US Olympic team.

In general, the outcome of any contest depends not only on the talent
and other given characteristics of the contestants, but also on how much
effort they expend and on how much they invest in performance enhancement. Former tennis great John McEnroe once complained that
he had more talent in his little finger than archrival Ivan Lendl had in

his whole body. Maybe so, but Lendl's strict training regimen and long hours on the practice courts nonetheless enabled him to displace McEnroe from the top of the tennis rankings.

Few people responded sympathetically to McEnroe's graceless complaint, and even many of his most ardent fans could not help having admired Lendl's dedication. Why, then, is investment in performance enhancement something that people might wish to inhibit by social norms and other means?

In some cases — the consumption of anabolic steroids by athletes, for example — the answer appears obvious: namely, that the investment is costly and adds nothing of genuine value. On the cost side, athletes incur not only the monetary outlays needed for purchasing the drug, they also face potentially severe health consequences. In the short term, these include hair loss, skin disorders, heightened aggressiveness, and even severe psychosis. In the long term, there is at least fragmentary evidence linking steroid consumption to a variety of circulatory disorders, testicular atrophy, and higher risks of some cancers (Windsor and Dumitru 1988).

Individual athletes are willing to endure these costs because the drugs enhance performance. According to one estimate, for example, steroid use provides a half-second advantage for a 100-meter sprinter, more than eight times the average winning margin in the three most recent Olympic Games.

And yet there is no evidence whatever that steroid use enhances the value of athletic competition from a spectator's perspective. National Football League fans, for example, have little reason to prefer that opposing linemen average 300 pounds rather than 250. Of course, the advantage of larger players to any individual team can be decisive. Thus, the starting offensive linemen on the 1996 Super Bowl Champion Dallas Cowboys averaged 333 pounds, some 30 pounds more than their counterparts on the Pittsburgh Steelers. And so, in the absence of effective drug testing, widespread ingestion of steroids, with all their attendant health risks, is inevitable. All parties — fans and athletes alike — would benefit if effective testing methods made it possible to eliminate steroid use entirely.

In other cases, investments in performance enhancement translate

TABLE 8.1
The Relationship between the Winner's Reward and Investment
in Performance-Enhancement

Winner's Investment in Performance Enhancement ($)	Value of the Winner's Prize
0	24
1	28
2	31
3	32
4	32.02
5	32.03

into a more valuable final product. The sopranos who compete for the handful of recording contracts issued each year spend thousands of dollars on voice coaches and other forms of music instruction. These efforts translate into greater clarity, dynamic range, and other performance characteristics that yield additional listener satisfaction.

In cases like these, society has an interest in performance enhancement, but only up to a point. The criterion for social efficiency in such cases is to invest as long as the next dollar spent raises the value of the winner's performance by at least one dollar. As the following examples will suggest, however, the incentives facing contestants tend to push investment far past the efficient level.

To illustrate the basic forces involved, I consider examples in which two identical contestants are vying for a prize whose value rises at a diminishing rate with the winner's investment in performance enhancement, as shown in table 8.1.

What is the socially optimal investment level given the relationship in table 8.1? The criterion stated above suggests that the first dollar spent on performance enhancement is clearly worthwhile, because it raises the winner's reward by $4, from $24 to $28. The second dollar spent is less effective, raising the winner's reward from $28 to $31, a gain of only $3. But this is still a net gain of $2 and hence worth doing. Raising the investment another dollar to $3 produces only an extra dollar of reward—from $31 to $32—and so, from a social perspective, it is worth doing, but only just. Note, finally, that the fourth dollar of investment raises the prize by only two cents, which would mean a net social loss of

98 cents. In this simple example, then, the socially optimal level of investment in performance enhancement is $3.

One immediate source of waste in examples of this sort is that if there were multiple contestants each investing $3, all but one of their investments would be superfluous. In this example with two contestants, there would thus be $3 of waste even if each contestant limited her investment to the socially optimal level. Waste of just this kind has been attributed to patent races, and several commentators have suggested that a more efficient result could be obtained if the government were simply to assign each development project to a separate laboratory (see, for example, Loury [1979]).

There are obvious problems with this proposal, however, not least among which is that the government is hardly in a position to know which laboratories are the most likely sources of yet uninvented technologies. So it may be that some duplication of effort is an unavoidable cost in many cases.

But even if we accept this cost, there is still another source of inefficiency when reward depends on rank. To begin with the most extreme case, suppose that whichever contestant invests the most in performance enhancement is certain to win the prize. (In the event of a tie, let the winner be chosen by the flip of a coin.) Suppose further that each of our two identical contestants has currently invested $3 in performance enhancement. Given the procedure for resolving ties, each thus has a 50 percent chance of winning, and thus an expected reward equal to 50 percent of $32, or $16.

Suppose each contestant then asks herself, "Does it pay to invest an extra dollar?" If she does so and her rival does not, she will win $32.02 with certainty. By contrast, if she does not invest and her rival does, she will have absolutely nothing to show for her $3 investment. So the incentives strongly favor each contestant investing another dollar. With both contestants now investing $4, each must decide whether to invest yet another dollar. Each knows that the extra dollar will increase the value of the winner's prize by only a penny. But again, each knows that if she invests and her rival does not, she will win the entire prize, $32.03, with certainty; and that if her rival invests while she does not, her own

$4 investment will have gone for naught. If both invest, each will have a 50 percent chance to win $32.03, or an expected reward of $16.015.

No matter what she expects her rival to do, if she could be sure the escalation would stop with the next round, it would be better for her to invest. Of course she cannot be sure that further escalation will not ensue, for at that point the incentives to invest further will be as compellingly attractive as before.

The term "entrapment model" has been used to describe the case in which the top investor wins the prize with probability 1. Laboratory experiments suggest that investments in performance enhancement reach astonishingly high levels under this incentive structure — as much as twenty times the value of the prize itself when the prize is worth $20 (Max Bazerman, personal communication).

The entrapment model is an extreme case. More generally, we would not expect the highest investor to be sure of winning. A popular alternative model in the literature on rent-seeking is the "lottery" model, so called because of its likeness to the way in which the odds in state lotteries are determined. In a lottery, someone who buys 10 percent of all tickets sold has a 10 percent chance of winning. Likewise, in the example with two identical contestants, the lottery scheme means that someone who invests three times as much as his rival has a 75 percent chance of being the winner. More generally, a contestant's probability of winning is equal to his share of total investment in performance enhancement. For present purposes, the critical difference between the lottery model and the entrapment model is that the incentives to escalate investment are weaker under the lottery model.

In the entrapment model, recall, if the two candidates had equal investments to begin with, either could tip the outcome decisively in her favor by making only a small additional investment. In the lottery model, by contrast, a slight increase in investment means only a slight increase in the odds of winning. Suppose, for example, that each candidate has $4 of investment initially, so that each initially has a 50 percent chance of winning in either model. In the entrapment model, if one candidate ups her investment to $5, her probability of winning soars to 100 percent. In the lottery model, by contrast, if one candidate invests an extra dollar, total investment will be $9, which means that her share of that total will be 5/9, or just less than 56 percent. Investing the extra dollar thus increases her probability of winning by less than 12 percent in the lottery model.

Although the incentives for escalating investment are much weaker in the lottery model than in the entrapment model, we see excessive investment in performance enhancement even in the lottery model. Returning to the example described in table 8.1, suppose each of our two contestants is currently spending $3 on performance enhancement. This means that each has a 50 percent chance of winning $32, or an expected payoff of $16. If one of them invests an extra dollar while the other remains at $3, the higher investor's share of total investment will be 4/7, or just over 57 percent. She will thus have a 57 percent chance of winning $32.02, which computes to an expected payoff of $18.30. And since this is more than one dollar better than her previous expected payoff, it pays to invest the extra dollar.

What about the other contestant? If she stays at $3 while her rival moves to $4, her odds of winning will fall to 3/7. This yields an expected payoff of only 13.72. If she, too, moves to $4, however, her odds of winning will again be 50 percent, which means an expected payoff of just over $16. And since that is more than a dollar higher than she expects from standing pat, it also pays her to invest the extra dollar.

The lottery model of investment has been well studied in the literature on rent-seeking and patent races (Congleton 1980; Frank and Cook 1993). When there are two identically situated contestants independently investing in pursuit of a fixed reward, each will invest one-fourth of that reward on performance enhancement. Together, they will thus squander one-half the total reward on mutually offsetting investments in performance enhancement. If there are not two contestants but N, each investing independently under the incentives of the lottery model, the total amount spent on performance enhancement will be $(N - 1)/N$. Thus, as the number of contestants grows, the level of total investment quickly approaches the value of the reward being sought. So even under the much weaker incentives posed by the lottery model, mutually offsetting investments in performance enhancement remain substantial.

Common sense, empirical observation, and theoretical analyses of investment incentives thus yield a common message: In contests in which investments in performance enhancement affect individual contestants' odds of winning, there will invariably be mutually offsetting, socially inefficient patterns of investment in performance enhancement.[1] Such investments bear an obvious resemblance to the purchase of armaments in the classic military arms race, and hence the term "positional arms race." And hence, too, the attraction of collective agreements to limit these arms races. Given the obvious incentives for contestants to violate these agreements, they are destined to fail unless there is considerable power to enforce them. Appreciating this difficulty, professional sports franchises cede much of their autonomy to league officials who impose team roster limits, revenue-sharing schemes, salary caps, and other measures that constrain investment in performance enhancement. In the business world, contracting parties often sign binding agreements that commit them to arbitration in the event of disputes. By so doing, they sacrifice the option of pursuing their interests as fully as they might wish to later, but in return they insulate themselves from costly legal battles. And with a similar goal in mind, a federal judge in South Dakota recently announced — presumably to the approval of litigants — that he would read only the first fifteen pages of any brief submitted before his court.

An Example: Social Norms That Limit Conspicuous Consumption

Many small towns have informal norms against conspicuous consumption. The power of these norms became vividly apparent to me several years ago when they led me to pass up what would otherwise have been an irresistible consumption opportunity. A relative in California had bought a new Porsche 911 Cabriolet during a visit to France. Because the franc was then trading cheaply against the dollar, he paid only $26,000 for essentially the same car that would have cost him $70,000 had he purchased it in the United States.

Actually, there was one important difference between the car he bought in Europe and the one he would have bought here. When he returned to California he discovered that he could not register his car there because it had been produced for the European market. California dealers had successfully lobbied for a law that made such cars illegal even if retrofitted to satisfy all California pollution regulations. As a stopgap measure, he registered it in Oregon, but in time this led to difficulty with his insurance company. . . .

In the end, he decided to sell the car. Being a family member, I had a chance to buy it for something like $15,000 (by that time it was three years old). And since my home state of New York does not prohibit retrofitting European car models, I could have owned and operated it in full compliance with the law.

I was sorely tempted. But as a resident of Ithaca, a small upstate town with strong norms against conspicuous consumption, it was simply not tenable for me to buy this car. I realized that unless I could put a sign on it that explained how I happened to acquire it, I would never feel comfortable driving it. I still wonder whether I made the right decision. But what is not in question is that there would have been a social price to pay if I had bought it. Of course, the particular consumption norms that a community adopts will depend not only on its size, but also on other factors like its income level and the degree of interpersonal contact between its members. An Ithaca-size community in Marin County, California, for example, would thus be unlikely to impose comparable social sanctions on its members who drive expensive automobiles.

Why do people want to discourage conspicuous consumption? And, given that they do, what forces enable them to succeed? The first question turns out to be easier than the second, so I consider it first. The short answer is that norms against conspicuous consumption are attractive because they help to avoid the costs of mine-is-bigger consumption arms races.

All available evidence tells us that satisfaction depends at least as much on relative consumption as on absolute consumption levels (for an extensive summary of this evidence, see Frank [1985, chap. 2]). The result is that consumers confront a positional arms race when they decide how to allocate their time between leisure and work. From the individual's perspective, giving up leisure time to work longer hours gives rise to two benefits: an increase in absolute consumption and an increase in relative consumption. From a collective perspective, however, the second of these benefits is spurious, for when everyone works longer hours, relative consumption levels remain unchanged: hence the utility of collective agreements to weaken incentives to work longer hours.

In the legal arena, one strategy is to penalize firms whose employees work more than a specified number of hours, as the Fair Labor Standards Act does through its overtime provisions. Less formally, the community can attempt to discourage consumption by the adoption of social norms against excessive consumption. Such norms, if enforceable, would enable people to spend more time with their families, to save more, and in other ways to achieve more balance in their lives.

The Enforcement Problem

How are social norms enforced? In particular, what sanctions can be brought to bear against those who violate them? And if these sanctions are costly to impose, what prevents potential enforcers from free-riding? As the late James Coleman observed (1990, chap. 10), the mere fact that a norm might be nice to have is by no means sufficient to bring about its existence. The demand for norms arises from externalities and other collective action problems, yet there are many externalities for which there are no corresponding norms.

In Coleman's view, the free-rider problem can be overcome through "connectedness," his term for closely linked networks of personal relationships. Thus, if A benefits from B's efforts to enforce a social norm, it may be possible for A to reward B with a favor in some other context. But even in small, close-knit communities, the reciprocal exchange of favors appears hardly sufficient to assure the enforcement of a social norm against conspicuous consumption.

In the exchange theory view, people associate with one another because — and only because — of the exchange benefits they expect to reap in the process. Someone who abstains from associating with the violator of a social norm thus punishes not only the violator but also himself. Suppose this cost deters a potential enforcer from taking action. Failure to enforce is itself an offense, but one that is both less serious and more difficult to observe than the original violation. Yet the costs required to punish this secondary offense will be on a par with those required to sanction the original violator. If that cost deterred potential enforcers in the first instance, it will perforce deter them from taking action against delinquent enforcers. And once it becomes known that delinquent enforcers face no discipline, the prospects for action against the original norm violators become even more tenuous.

On the adherence side of the norm market, there are similar contradictions, for we know that people often follow norms even when external sanctions are not a credible threat. For example, the norm to tip in restaurants is almost impossible to enforce by external sanctions in the case of people who eat at restaurants along interstate highways, yet the observed tipping rates in such restaurants are little different than those in restaurants patronized mostly by local diners.

An alternative approach is to suppose that both adherence to and enforcement of social norms are motivated not only by the material rewards and penalties inherent in exchange relationships but also by internal, nonmaterial rewards. Thus, people may incur costs to enforce social norms simply because it gives them satisfaction to take action against violators; similarly, people may follow social norms simply because they feel uncomfortable, even in the absence of material sanctions, when they violate them.

At first blush, this approach seems to abandon the discipline of the purposive rational actor model, a step that many rational choice theorists are understandably reluctant to take. Thus, as Coleman wrote: "To examine the process whereby norms are internalized is to enter waters that are treacherous for a theory grounded on rational choice. Asking the question of how individuals come to have the interests they exhibit is ordinarily not possible in constructing such a theory" (1990, chap. 11, 292).

Yet this is a step that behavioral scientists ultimately cannot avoid. In chapter 1, I argued that it is fruitful to view preferences, or internal motivational states, not just as ends in themselves, but as means for achieving important material objectives. Concern about relative wealth, for example, proves helpful in interpersonal bargaining contexts.

The logic behind this claim is illustrated by the ultimatum bargaining game, discussed in chapter 6. To recapitulate, the game begins with Proposer being given a sum of money (say, $100) that he must then propose how to divide between himself and Responder. Responder then has two options: 1) he can accept, in which case each party gets the amount proposed; or 2) he can refuse, in which case each party gets zero and the $100 goes back to the experimenter.

If Proposer believes that Responder cares only about absolute wealth, his own wealth-maximizing strategy is clear: he should propose $99 for himself and $1 for Responder (only integer dollar amounts are allowed). If Proposer's assumption about Responder is correct, Responder will accept this one-sided offer because he will reason that getting $1 is better than getting nothing.

But suppose Proposer believed that Responder cares not only about absolute but also relative wealth levels. Responder might then refuse the one-sided offer, even though he stands to gain from it in absolute terms, because he finds the relative terms so distasteful. The irony is that the effect of Proposer's believing that Responder cares about relative wealth is to substantially boost the amount that Proposer offers Responder. By virtue of his concern about relative wealth, Responder becomes a much more effective bargainer.

But this benefit comes at a cost. In the context of the ultimatum bargaining game, for example, if Proposer miscalculates and does make a one-sided proposal, Responder will incur the cost of refusing it. Likewise, someone who cares about relative position may willingly incur the cost of sanctioning the violator of a consumption norm, whereas someone who cared only about absolute wealth would not incur this cost. But the latter person would also be a much less effective bargainer in other contexts.

As a descriptive matter, it is clear that most people have at least a limited willingness to incur costs both to enforce and to adhere to social norms. And so there are neither compelling theoretical nor empirical grounds for insisting that implementation of social norms be rooted only in mutually beneficial exchange relationships.

Of course, considerations of exchange need not be excluded from the implementation of social norms. Indeed, the same internal motivations that lead a person to incur the costs of sanctioning the violator of a social norm are likely also to help cement alliances with others who incur these costs. In practice, then, internal motivations and exchange relationships will often act in mutually reinforcing ways. This observation may help explain why a norm against conspicuous consumption has considerably more force in small communities than in large urban areas.

The importance of internal motivations is attested to by the resources devoted to efforts aimed at molding these motivations. Thus, a portion of the curriculum in public schools is devoted to inculcating the duties of citizenship. A major purpose of organized religion is to help foster the development of feelings that promote social behavior and inhibit antisocial behavior. Similar themes receive consistent emphasis in political campaign rhetoric. And as Edward Banfield (1958) has observed, the societies that succeed in these efforts appear far more likely than others to succeed in the economic domain, as well.

FURTHER EXAMPLES

The Academy Award–winning film *Chariots of Fire* portrays British collegiate track and field competitors who have developed an implicit norm that limits their training and practice time. Their apparent understanding is that since the most talented runner will win whether all train arduously or none does, the sensible thing is for no one to train very hard. This arrangement is challenged by an outsider with a rigorous training regimen. In response, the incumbents bring considerable social pressure to bear upon the maverick. In the face of such pressure, most normal challengers might have succumbed. But this particular runner is tough, and he goes on to win in the end.

This is not to say that the social norm he helped to destroy in the process was a desirable one. Deciding races on the basis of talent alone may be efficient, but it is not necessarily fair. The underlying distribution of running talent, after all, is essentially a matter of luck. Even so, many of us who believe that effort should also matter are troubled by the types of effort that emerge when competition is completely unregulated.

Norms against Exceeding Piece-Rate Quotas

Social norms for curtailing effort are also common on the shop floor. In many manufacturing and sales jobs, it is possible to measure with reasonable precision what each worker produces. According to traditional economic theory, such conditions strongly favor the use of piece-rate pay schemes, which reward workers in direct proportion to the amounts they produce. One of the enduring puzzles in labor economics is the relative scarcity of these schemes. Even in sales, perhaps the easiest activity in which to monitor productivity, a National Industrial Conference Board study found that more than half of all compensation plans imposed caps on total sales commissions (1970, 79). Similar pay ceilings are described in a large literature that examines the widespread practice whereby workers on piece rates establish their own informal production quotas and impose strong sanctions against those who violate them (for a survey of this literature, see Frank [1985, chap. 5]). Cases have even been reported in which firms themselves impose limits on production.

Worker-imposed production quotas have been described as devices whereby workers fool management about the difficulty of their production tasks, in the fear that if they earn too much under existing piece rates, management will simply lower the rates (Whyte 1955, 201). In support of this interpretation, the sociologist Donald Roy describes the following conversation, in which Starkey, an experienced worker, counsels Tennessee, a new man on the job, on the need to work slowly when under the gaze of the time-study man:

> "Another thing," said Starkey, "you were running that job too damn fast before they timed you on it! I was watching you yesterday . . . "
>
> "I don't see how I could have run it any slower," said Tennessee. "I stood there like I was practically paralyzed!"
>
> "Remember those bastards are paid to screw you," said Starkey. "And that's all they think about. They'll stay up half the night figuring out how to beat you out of a dime. They figure you're going to try to fool them, so they make allowances for that. They set the prices low enough to allow for what you do."
>
> "Well, then, what the hell chance have I got?" asked Tennessee.
>
> "It's up to you to figure out how to fool them more than they allow for," said Starkey.
>
> "The trouble with me is I get nervous with that guy standing in back of me, and I can't think," said Tennessee.
>
> "You just haven't had enough experience yet," said Starkey. "Wait until you have been here a couple of years and you'll do your best think-

ing when those guys are standing behind you." (Roy, quoted in Whyte [1955, 15])

It would be foolish not to suppose that workers slow down when the time-study man visits the factory to establish quotas for piece rates. Yet to suppose that management has no way to discover that a quota has been set too low is to credit management with none of the ingenuity demonstrated by workers in their skirmishes with the time-study man. In fact, management has ample means for discovering how much time production tasks require. Thus, one older study describes an electrical assembly plant strike during which supervisors were easily able to double existing production quotas (Mangum 1964, 48).

There are other cases in which management clearly knew that workers could easily exceed their production quotas. In one factory, for example, workers routinely met their quotas by mid-afternoon and spent the remainder of their workday playing cards in the restrooms, prompting several wives to complain to management about their husbands' gambling losses (Mangum 1964, 48).

So if these quotas substantially understate what workers are capable of producing, and management knows it, why doesn't management elicit higher production by simply reducing current piece rates? Management's implicit tolerance of production quotas makes much more sense if we interpret such agreements as social norms whereby workers attempt to curb positional arms races with one another. The difficulty is that if each worker's chances of promotion depend in part on relative productivity, the conditions are ripe for a mutually offsetting effort pattern. Each worker attempts to produce more in the hope of gaining ground relative to the others, yet when all workers double their efforts, relative promotion prospects remain largely the same. From a collective vantage point, the extra output summoned by unregulated piece rates is not sufficient to compensate for the extra effort required to produce it. When promotion prospects depend on relative effort, social enforcement of informal production quotas may bring private incentives more in line with collective interests.

Nerd Norms

We also see social norms against excess effort in the world of education. Consider, for example, the positional arms race that arises when students are graded on the curve. From students' perspective, grading on the curve makes extra effort more attractive to each individual student than it is to students as a whole, for if all students increase their efforts in an attempt to improve their grades, the aggregate grade distribution will remain much the same as before.

Whether a positional arms race is inefficient depends, of course, on the perspective from which it is viewed. Students think grading on the curve leads to excessive effort. Parents and teachers, by contrast, are more likely to view the competitive struggle for higher grades as benign. Recalling their own youth, many are inclined to believe that students would tend to spend far too little time on their studies in the absence of competitive pressures. In their view, a positional arms race is just what the doctor ordered.

It is not surprising, then, that different social norms about academic effort have evolved among students, on the one hand, and concerned adults, on the other. Students are quick to brand as "nerds" or social misfits those among them who "study too hard" or attempt to curry favor with teachers. Parents and teachers, for their part, try to counter this norm with norms of their own that extol the virtues of academic achievement.

Sabbath Norms

Judaism, Christianity, and other religions of the world embrace Sabbath norms, which enjoin practitioners to set aside a day each week for rest and worship. Such norms may be viewed as early precursors of blue laws, which mobilized the state's enforcement powers toward similar ends. Each may plausibly be seen as a device for limiting the extent to which people can trade leisure time for additional income. To the extent that utility depends strongly on relative income, Sabbath norms and blue laws thus help bring individual and collective incentives into closer alignment.

Norms Governing Dueling

In centuries past, a European gentleman's response to a profound insult was to challenge the offending party to a duel. Accompanied by their seconds, the antagonists would typically assemble at dawn for their contest, which was governed by several formal rules. On examination, each of these rules is most plausibly interpreted as a positional arms-control agreement.

One rule, for example, specified the physical distance between the antagonists at the actual moment of the duel itself. It called for them to stand back to back, then march off a given number of paces before each turned to fire. The transparent purpose of this rule was to reduce the odds of the participants being killed. Establishing physical separation between the duelists made it more likely that their shots would miss than if they simply turned and fired at point-blank range.

A second rule governed the characteristics of the guns employed. Among other things, it specified that the interior surfaces of the barrels of the guns be smooth, as opposed to having spiral grooves; and it called for weapons that fired only a single shot. The purpose of requiring smooth gun barrels was to make the trajectories of the bullets less true. "Rifling" — the engraving of spiral grooves on the inner surface of a gun barrel — imparts a spin to the bullet as it leaves the weapon. This causes the bullet to follow a much straighter trajectory than it would if the barrel had been smooth, much as a football thrown with a tight spiral tends to be more accurate than one without. Projectiles that lack spin tend to wobble and flutter erratically, like the knuckleball in baseball. To appreciate the utility of the single-shot restriction, we need only contemplate the hypothetical fate of duelists who faced off with 100-shot assault rifles.

These restrictions served their intended purpose. Thus, one study of some two-hundred British duels concluded that only one in six duelists was even hit by his opponent's bullet, and only one in fourteen was killed (Wilkinson 1979, 45–46). These figures probably overstate the true casualty rates, since "very many duels which left no business for the coroner must have gone unregistered" (Kiernan 1988, 144). Yet even these odds were a high price to pay for defending one's honor. And indeed, virtually all industrial societies have now made dueling illegal.

Fashion Norms

Many social norms regarding dress and fashion may also be interpreted plausibly as positional arms-control agreements. This claim springs from the well-documented finding in experimental psychology that perception and evaluation are strongly dependent on the observer's frame of reference (Helson 1964). Consider, for instance, the person who wishes to make a fashion statement that he or she is among the avant garde, someone on the cutting edge. In some American social circles during the 1950s, that could be accomplished by wearing pierced earrings. But as more and more people adopted this practice, it ceased to communicate avant-garde status. At the same time, those who wanted to make a conservative fashion statement gradually became more free to wear pierced earrings.

For a period during the 1960s and 1970s, one could be on fashion's cutting edge by wearing two pierced earrings in one earlobe. But by the 1990s multiple ear piercings had lost much of their social significance, the threshold of cutting-edge status having drifted to upwards of a dozen pierced earrings, or a smaller number of piercings of the nose, eyebrows, or other parts of the body. A similar escalation has taken place in the number, size, and placement of tattoos that define avant-garde status.

There is unlikely, however, to have been any corresponding increase in the value of avant-garde fashion status to those who desire it. Being in the right-hand tail of the fashion distribution means pretty much the same now as it once did. So to the extent that there are costs associated with body piercings, tattoos, and other steps required to achieve avant-garde status, the current situation is wasteful compared to the earlier one, which required fewer steps. In this sense, the erosion of social norms against tattoos and body piercings has given rise to a social loss. Of course, the costs associated with this loss are small in most cases. Yet since each body piercing carries with it a small risk of infection, the costs will continue to rise as the number of piercings rises. And once these costs reach a certain threshold, support may again mobilize on behalf of social norms that discourage body mutilation.

Similar cycles occur with respect to behaviors considered to be in bad taste. In the 1950s, for example, prevailing norms prevented major national magazines from accepting ads that used nude photographs to draw readers' attention. Advertisers naturally have powerful incentives to chip away at these norms, for they must compete vigorously for the buyer's limited attention. And, indeed, norms regarding good taste have evolved in a way similar to those regarding body mutilation.

Consider, for instance, the evolution of perfume ads. First came the nude silhouette; then increasingly well-lighted and detailed nude photographs; and more recently, photographs of what appear to be group sex acts. Each innovation achieved just the desired effect—drawing the reader's instant and rapt attention. Inevitably, however, competing advertisers have followed suit and the effect has been merely to shift our sense of what is considered attention-grabbing. Photographs that once would have shocked readers now often draw little more than a bored glance.

Whether this is a good thing or a bad thing naturally depends on one's view about public nudity. Many believe that the earlier, stricter norms were ill advised in the first place, the legacy of a more prudish and repressive era. And yet even those who take this view also are likely to believe that there are some kinds of photographic material that ought not to be used in advertisements in national magazines. Where this limit lies will obviously differ a great deal from person to person. And each person's threshold of discomfort will depend in part on the standards currently in observance. But we should not be surprised that as advertisers continue to break new ground in their struggle to capture our attention, the point may come when social forces again mobilize in favor of stricter standards of "public decency." Such forces are yet another example of a positional arms-control agreement.

Norms against Vanity

A similar claim can be made on behalf of social norms that discourage cosmetic surgery. Cosmetic and/or reconstructive surgery has produced dramatic benefits for many people. It has enabled badly disfigured accident victims to recover a more normal appearance and so to continue with their lives. It has also eliminated the extreme self-consciousness felt by people born with strikingly unusual or unattractive features. Such

surgery, however, is by no means confined to the conspicuously disfigured. "Normal" people are increasingly seeking surgical improvements
in their appearance. There were some six million cosmetic "procedures"
done in 2001, eighteen times the number just two decades earlier
(*www.plasticsurgery.org*). Once carefully guarded secrets, these procedures are now offered as prizes in charity raffles in southern California.

In individual cases, cosmetic surgery may be just as beneficial as reconstructive surgery is for accident victims. Buoyed by the confidence of
having a straight nose or a wrinkle-free complexion, patients sometimes
go on to achieve much more than they ever thought possible.

But the growing use of cosmetic surgery also has an unintended side
effect — it has altered our standards for normal appearance. A nose that
would once have seemed only slightly larger than average may now
seem jarringly big; the same person who once would have looked like an
average 55-year-old may now look nearly 70; and someone who once
would have been described as having slightly thinning hair or an average
amount of cellulite may now feel compelled to undergo hair transplanta-
tion or liposuction. Because such procedures shift our frame of reference, their payoffs to individuals are misleadingly large, and from a social perspective, reliance on them is therefore likely to be excessive.

It is difficult to imagine legal sanctions against cosmetic surgery as a
remedy for this problem. But at least some communities embrace powerful social norms against cosmetic surgery, heaping scorn and ridicule on
the consumers of face lifts and tummy tucks. In individual cases, these
norms may seem cruel. And yet, without them, many more people might
feel compelled to bear the risk and expense of cosmetic surgery.

The Breakdown of Social Norms

For most of the history of print journalism, and for the first several decades of
electronic journalism, there were strong social norms opposing the exploita-
tion of lurid or sensational news stories. Thus, as recently as the early 1960s,
journalists abided by a tacit agreement not to publicize a sitting American
president's flagrant acts of marital infidelity. By the 1990s, needless to say,
such topics had become fair game, not only in the tabloid press but also in
mainstream news outlets. Why this dramatic transformation?

One important change has been an increase in the economic incentives to violate implicit norms. Television executives, for example, now realize that a top-rated news program is an important ingredient for a successful schedule of prime time programming, whose advertising revenues now measure in the hundreds of millions of dollars. And newspaper editors, for their part, recognize the growing trend for the most popular local paper to capture the entire market.

Another important change in recent years has been the movement toward more open competition for audiences. In television, this has resulted from the proliferation of cable and satellite services, as well as the addition of a fourth major broadcast network. The print media, for their part, have faced growing competition from television, from magazines targeted at specialty audiences, and from the addition of one new national newspaper (*USA Today*) and the increased availability of two others (the *New York Times* and the *Wall Street Journal*).

Both the larger prizes and the more competitive environment have worked in tandem to fuel the growing trend toward sensationalism. In the past, a relatively small number of competitors interacted repeatedly with one another. With only three television networks, a small number of movie studios, and a handful of major publishers, it was possible for the news and entertainment industries to implement implicit social norms about the kind of material that could be shown or written about. The fact that the prizes were relatively small, moreover, kept the temptation to violate these norms within reasonable limits.

Thus, each publisher knew it could make extra profits in the short run by publishing lurid books or reporting candidates' sexual indiscretions. But each also knew that the advantage would be short-lived because its defection would spell the breakdown of their implicit agreements. And in the smaller markets of yesteryear, the potential gains from breaking ranks were not all that large anyway. In today's competitive climate, such restraint has proved virtually impossible to sustain. There is simply too much at stake and too many peripheral actors with little to lose.

Many of the same forces that have undermined social norms in the news media have undermined norms in other arenas as well. For example, just as the top prizes have escalated in the news media, so, too, have the top prizes in the labor market overall. During the last two decades, for example, the top 1 percent of U.S. earners have captured more than 40 percent of all earnings growth.

Personal injury lawyers who used to file lawsuits seeking $10,000 damage payments for clients with stiff necks now head up teams that compete for a share of multibillion dollar class-action judgments. Can anyone doubt that the decorum of lawyers competing for such prizes is little constrained by social norms?

CEOs who earned thirty times as much as the average worker twenty years ago now earn more than four hundred times as much. The top performers' salaries have also escalated sharply in sales, journalism, medicine, dentistry, design, and even academia. With such large rewards at stake, social norms are increasingly less able to restrain individual interest.

Changes in the reward structure in private markets have indirect as well as direct effects on the enforceability of social norms. By "direct effect," I mean that when the monetary payoff for violating a norm increases, a rational actor becomes more likely to violate it. But holding payoffs and other relevant factors constant, the willingness to obey a norm is also indirectly influenced by the overall frequency with which people comply with it. Because they entail potentially explosive positive-feedback processes, the indirect effects often turn out to be far more important than the direct effects. Thus, when a change in payoffs leads marginal actors to violate a social norm, their defections lead others also to violate that norm, and these defections have ramifications of their own. In this manner, seemingly trivial changes in direct financial incentives may result in the complete breakdown of specific social norms.

Concluding Remarks

In the widget factory, long a staple in economics textbooks, reward depends only on absolute performance. A worker who assembles ten widgets per hour, for example, will be paid only half as much as a one who assembles twenty. More commonly, however, reward depends not only on absolute performance but on relative performance. Reward by rank almost invariably gives rise to escalating patterns of mutually offsetting investments undertaken by rivals jockeying for position. Such positional arms races, examples of which include advertising campaigns, consumption of performance-enhancing drugs, and cram courses for the SATs, are a conspicuous feature of the economic landscape. Like military arms races, positional arms races are often wasteful. In addition to such formal positional arms-control agreements as random drug testing of athletes and chronological age mandates for kindergarten students, less formal mechanisms such as social norms and moral suasion have also been employed to curb wasteful battles for position, as when students attempt to ostracize classmates who study too hard, or when news organizations implicitly agree not to dwell on sensational or lurid news stories.

NOTES

1. An important potential exception to this claim involves cases where the prize being sought substantially understates the social value of the winner's performance. In such cases, investment in performance enhancement may be insufficient despite the reward-by-rank payoff structure. In other cases, insufficient effort may be the expected result if it is too costly for employers to prevent shirking through direct monitoring of worker behavior. In these cases, employers and employees may gain through the artificial creation of a positional arms race — as in compensation schemes based in part on relative performance.

9

Does Studying Economics Inhibit Cooperation?

IN AN ESSAY written in 1879, Francis Amasa Walker tried to explain "why economists tend to be in bad odor amongst real people." Walker, who went on to become the first president of the American Economic Association, argued that it was partly because economists disregard "the customs and beliefs that tie individuals to their occupations and locations and lead them to act in ways contrary to the predictions of economic theory" (quoted by Robert Solow, as reported in the *Chronicle of Higher Education*, 8 January, 1986).

More than a century later, public skepticism toward economists remains. At least some of it appears to be rooted in the perception that the economist's narrow self-interest model encourages people to disregard the interests of others. In this chapter I will summarize evidence that is consistent with this perception.

ECONOMISTS AND THE SELF-INTEREST MODEL

If pressed, most economists will concede that people sometimes care about more than just their own material well-being. Many have concerns for the welfare of other people, for aesthetics, for their duties as citizens, and so on.

Yet few economists include these broader concerns in their models of human behavior. It may well be that the unpaid volunteer who heads the local United Way campaign is driven purely by his concern for the disadvantaged; but economists feel on much firmer ground if they can identify some more narrowly self-interested motive for his action.

The self-interest model has well-established explanatory power. Whatever role love may play in sustaining marriage relationships, we know that divorce rates are higher in states that provide more liberal welfare benefits. When energy prices rise, people are more likely to form car pools and to insulate their houses. When the opportunity cost of time rises, people have fewer children. And so on. From the economist's perspective, motives other than self-interest may matter, but they are peripheral to the main thrust of human endeavor, and we indulge them at our peril.

From its base in economics, the self-interest model has made strong inroads into a variety of other disciplines. Psychologists, political scientists, sociologists, philosophers, game theorists, biologists, and others rely increasingly on this model to explain and predict human behavior. (I should note, however, that recent years have seen a growing insurgency movement in the social sciences emphasizing the importance of non-egoistic motives. See, in particular the influential recent books by Etzioni [1988] and Mansbridge [1990].)

In this chapter I summarize the results of a study in which two colleagues and I investigated whether exposure to the self-interest model alters the extent to which people behave in self-interested ways (Frank, Gilovich, and Regan 1993a). The chapter is organized into two parts. In the first, I report the results of a series of empirical studies — some our own, some by other investigators — that support the hypothesis that economists behave in more self-interested ways. By itself, this evidence does not demonstrate that exposure to the self-interest model is the *cause* of more self-interested behavior, although, as we will see, a case can be made for this proposition on a priori grounds. An alternative interpretation is that economists may simply have been more self-interested to begin with, and this difference was one reason they chose to study economics. In the second part of the paper, I summarize evidence suggesting that exposure to the self-interest model does in fact increase self-interested behavior.

Do Economists Behave Differently?

The Free-Rider Experiments

One of the clearest predictions of the self-interest model is that people will tend to free-ride on the efforts of others when it comes to the provision of public or collective goods. Even people who would strongly benefit from having, say, higher program quality on public television have little incentive to contribute. After all, any single individual's contribution is far too small to alter the likelihood of achieving the desired outcome.

A study by Gerald Marwell and Ruth Ames (1981) found that students of economics are indeed much more likely to free-ride in experiments that called for private contributions to public goods. Their basic experiment involved a group of subjects who were given an initial endowment of money, which they were to allocate between two accounts, one "public," the other "private." Money deposited in a subject's private account was returned dollar for dollar to the subject at the end of the experiment. Money deposited in the public account was first pooled, then multiplied by some factor greater than one, and then distributed equally among all subjects.

Under these circumstances, the socially optimal behavior is for each subject to put her entire endowment in the public account. But individually the most advantageous strategy is to put all of it in the private account. The self-interest model predicts that all subjects will follow the latter strategy. Most don't. Across eleven replications of the experiment, the average contribution to the public account was approximately 49 percent.

It was only in a twelfth replication with first-year graduate students in economics as subjects that Marwell and Ames obtained results more nearly consistent with the self-interest model. These subjects contributed an average of only 20 percent of their initial endowments to the public account, a figure significantly less than the corresponding figure for noneconomists.

On completion of each replication of the experiment, Marwell and Ames asked their subjects two follow-up questions:

1. What is a "fair" investment in the public good?
2. Are you concerned about "fairness" in making your investment decision?

In response to the first question, 75 percent of the noneconomists answered "half or more" of the endowment, and 25 percent answered "all." In response to the second question, almost all noneconomists answered "yes." The corresponding responses of the economics graduate students were much more difficult to summarize. As Marwell and Ames wrote,

> More than one-third of the economists either refused to answer the question regarding what is fair, or gave very complex, uncodable responses. It seems that the meaning of "fairness" in this context was somewhat alien for this group. Those who did respond were much more likely to say that little or no contribution was "fair." In addition, the economics graduate students were about half as likely as other subjects to indicate that they were "concerned with fairness" in making their decisions. (1981, 309)

The Marwell and Ames study can be criticized on the grounds that their noneconomist control groups consisted of high school students and college undergraduates, who differ in a variety of ways from first-year graduate students in any discipline. Perhaps the most obvious difference is age. As we will see, however, criticism based on the age difference is blunted by our own evidence that older students generally give greater weight to social concerns like the ones that arise in free-rider experiments. It remains possible, however, that more mature students might have had a more sophisticated understanding of the nuances and ambiguities inherent in concepts like fairness, and for that reason gave less easily coded responses to the follow-up questions.

Yet another concern with the Marwell and Ames experiments is not easily dismissed. Although the authors do not report the sex composition of their group of economics graduate students, such groups are almost always preponderantly male. The authors' control groups of high school and undergraduate students, by contrast, consisted equally of males and females. (This was the case, in any event, for the groups whose sex composition the authors reported.) In the experiments that Gilovich, Regan, and I conducted, there was a sharp tendency for males to behave less cooperatively in experiments of this sort. So while the Marwell and Ames findings are suggestive, they do not clearly establish that economists behave differently.

Economists and the Ultimatum Bargaining Game

The other major study of whether economists behave differently from members of other disciplines is by John Carter and Michael Irons (1991).

These authors measured the self-interestedness of economists by examining their behavior in the ultimatum bargaining game described in chapter 6. Again, this simple game has two players, "Proposer" and "Responder." Proposer is given a sum of money (in these experiments, $10), and must then propose how to divide this sum between herself and Responder. Suppose Proposer offers $X for herself and the remaining $(10-X) for Responder. Once Proposer makes this offer, Responder has two choices: (1) she may accept, in which case each player gets the amount proposed; or (2) she may refuse, in which case each player gets zero. The game is played only once by the same partners.

If both players behave according to the self-interest model, the model makes an unequivocal prediction about how the game will proceed. Assuming the money cannot be divided into units smaller than one cent, Proposer will offer $9.99 for herself and the remaining $0.01 for Responder, and Responder will accept on the grounds that a penny is better than nothing. Since the game will not be repeated, there is no point in Responder turning down a low offer in the hope of generating a better offer in the future. Other researchers have shown that the strategy predicted by the self-interest model is almost never followed in practice: 50–50 splits are the most common outcome, and most one-sided offers are rejected out of concerns about fairness (Guth, Schmittberger, and Schwarze 1982; Kahneman, Knetsch, and Thaler 1986).

The research strategy employed by Carter and Irons was to compare the performance of economics majors and other students and see which group came closer to the predictions of the self-interest model. In a sample of 43 economics majors, the average minimum amount acceptable by Responder was $1.70, as compared with an average of $2.44 for a sample of 49 noneconomics majors. As Responders then, economics majors came significantly closer than nonmajors to the behavior predicted by the self-interest model.

In Proposer's role, as well, economics majors performed more in accordance with the predictions of the self-interest model than did nonmajors. Economics proposed to keep an average of $6.15 for themselves, as compared to an average of only $5.44 for the sample of 49 nonmajors.

Kahneman, Knetsch, and Thaler (1986) report findings similar to those of Carter and Irons: commerce students (the term used to describe business students in Canadian universities) were more likely than psychology students to make one-sided offers in ultimatum bargaining games.

One difficulty with the Carter and Irons results is that the way they assigned Proposer and Responder roles leaves open possible differences in the interpretation of what behavior is required in the name of fairness. In particular, Proposers earned their role by having achieved higher scores on a preliminary word game.[1] Proposers might thus reason that they were entitled to a greater share of the surplus on the strength of their earlier performance. The observed differences in the behavior of economics majors and nonmajors might therefore be ascribed to a differential tendency to attach significance to the earlier performance differences. The training received by economics students in the marginal productivity theory of wages lends at least surface plausibility to this interpretation.

To summarize the existing literature, both the Marwell and Ames and Carter and Irons studies provide evidence consistent with the hypothesis that economists tend to behave less cooperatively than noneconomists. But because of the specific experimental design problems mentioned, neither study is conclusive. In the following sections I describe how my colleagues and I attempted to test the hypothesis that economists behave less cooperatively.

Survey Data on Charitable Giving

The central role of the free-rider hypothesis in modern economic theory suggests that economists might be less likely than others to make gifts to private charities. To explore this possibility, we mailed questionnaires to 1,245 college professors randomly chosen from the professional directories of twenty-three disciplines, asking them to report the annual dollar amounts they gave to a variety of private charities. We received 576 responses with sufficient detail for inclusion in our study. Respondents were grouped into the following disciplines: economics ($N = 75$); other social sciences ($N = 106$); math, computer science, and engineering ($N = 48$); natural sciences ($N = 98$); humanities ($N = 94$); architecture, art, and music ($N = 68$); and professional ($N = 87$). (The "other social sciences" category includes psychology, sociology, political science, and anthropology; "natural sciences" includes physics, chemistry, biology, and geology; "humanities" includes philosophy, history, English, foreign languages, and religion; and "professional" includes education, business, and nursing.)

Members of every discipline, even economics, fell far short of the prediction of the strong version of the free-rider hypothesis. But the proportion of pure free-riders among economists (that is, those who reported giving no money to any charity) was more than double that of any of the other six areas included in the survey. (See figure 9.1.)

Although we do not have data on the gender of each survey respondent, gender differences by discipline do not appear to account for the pattern of free-ridership shown in figure 9.1. For example, the natural sciences, which are also preponderantly male, had only one-third as many free-riders as did economics.

Despite their generally higher incomes, economists were also among the least generous in terms of their median gifts to large charities like viewer-supported television and the United Way, which are shown in figures 9.2 and 9.3, respectively.

In fairness to the self-interest model, I should again acknowledge that there may be self-interested reasons for contributing even in the case of charities like the United Way and public television (see chapter 7). United Way campaigns, for example, are usually organized in the workplace and there is often considerable social pressure to contribute. Public television fund drives often make on-the-air announcements of donors' names and economists stand to benefit just as much as the members of any other discipline from being hailed as community-minded citizens. In the case of smaller, more personal charitable organizations, there are often even more compelling self-interested reasons for giving. After all, failure to contribute in accordance with one's financial ability may mean outright exclusion from the substantial private benefits associated with membership in religious groups, fraternal organizations, and the like.

An examination of economists' gifts to other charities revealed that their median annual gift is actually slightly larger, in absolute terms, than the median for all disciplines taken as a whole. But because economists have significantly higher salaries than do the members of most other disciplines, these data, like the data shown in figures 9.2 and 9.3, tend to

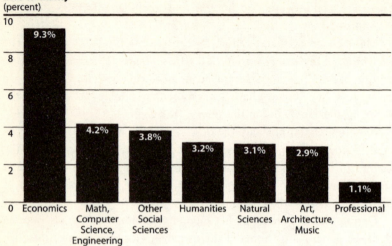

Figure 9.1 Proportion of Pure Free-Riders in Seven Disciplines

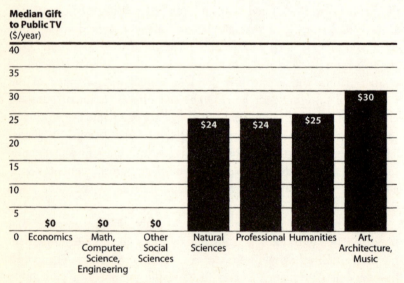

Figure 9.2 Median Gift to Public Television

**Median Gift
to United Way**
($/year)

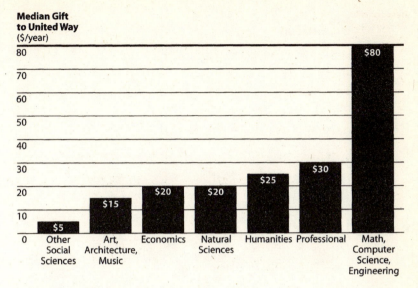

Figure 9.3 Median Gift to the United Way

overstate the relative generosity of economists. Unfortunately, we do not have direct income measures for the respondents in our survey, but we do have the number of years each respondent has been a practitioner in his or her discipline. In an attempt to take income effects into account, we estimated earnings functions (salary vs. years of experience) for each discipline using data from a large private university. We then applied the estimated coefficients from these earnings functions to the experience data from our survey to impute an income estimate for each respondent in our survey. Finally, we used these imputed income figures, together with our respondents' reports of their total charitable giving to estimate the relationship between income and total giving shown in figure 9.4. In the latter exercise, all economists were dropped from the sample on the grounds that our objective was to see whether the giving pattern of economists deviates from the pattern we see for other disciplines.

Thus, for example, in figure 9.4 we see that a noneconomist with an annual income of $44,000 (roughly, the median imputed income for architects in our sample) is expected to give almost $900 per year to charity, while a noneconomist with an income of $62,000 (roughly, the

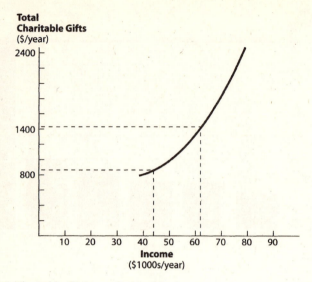

Figure 9.4 Charitable Giving vs. Imputed Income

median imputed income for economists in our sample) is expected to give more than $1,400 per year.

Using the relationship between charitable giving and income, we calculated the expected gift for each respondent as a function of his or her imputed income. We then calculated our measure of a discipline's generosity as the ratio of the average value of gifts actually reported by members of the discipline to the average value of gifts expected on the basis of the members' imputed incomes. A discipline is thus more generous than expected if this ratio exceeds 1.0, and less generous if it is less than 1.0. The computed ratio for economists was .91, which means that economists in our sample gave 91 percent as much as they would have been expected to give on the basis of their imputed incomes. The performance of economists by this measure is compared with the performance of other disciplines in figure 9.5.

On a number of other dimensions covered in our survey, the behavior of economists was little different from the behavior of members of other disciplines. For example, economists were only marginally less likely than members of other disciplines to report that they would take costly

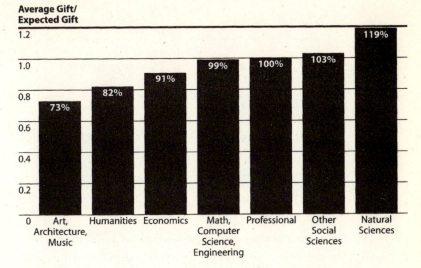

Figure 9.5 The Ratio of Average Gift to Gift Expected on the Basis of Income

administrative action to prosecute a student suspected of cheating. Economists were actually slightly above average for the entire sample in terms of the numbers of hours they reportedly spend in "volunteer activities." In terms of their reported frequency of voting in presidential elections, economists were only slightly below the sample average.

ECONOMISTS AND THE PRISONER'S DILEMMA

This section reports our results from a large experimental study of how economics majors and nonmajors perform in the prisoner's dilemma game. Figure 9.6 shows the monetary payoffs in dollars to two players in a standard prisoner's dilemma. In figure 9.6, as in all prisoner's dilemmas, each player gets a higher payoff when each cooperates than when each defects. But when one player's strategy is fixed, the other player always gets a higher payoff by defecting than by cooperating; and hence the dilemma. By following individual self-interest, each player does worse than if each had cooperated.

One of the most celebrated and controversial predictions of the self-

Your Partner

	Cooperate	Defect
Cooperate	$2 for your partner $2 for you	$3 for your partner $0 for you
Defect	$0 for your partner $3 for you	$1 for your partner $1 for you

(left side label: **You**, with "Cooperate" and "Defect" rows)

Figure 9.6 Monetary Payoffs for a Prisoner's Dilemma Game

interest model is that people will always defect in one-shot prisoner's dilemmas. The game thus provides an opportunity to examine the extent to which various groups exhibit self-interested behavior. Accordingly, we conducted a large one-shot prisoner's dilemma experiment involving both economics majors and nonmajors. Many of our subjects were students recruited from courses in which the prisoner's dilemma was an item on the syllabus. Others were given a detailed briefing about the game.

Our subjects met in groups of three and each was told that he would play the game once with each of the other two subjects. The payoff matrix, shown in figure 9.6, was the same for each play of the game. Subjects were told that the games would be played for real money, and that none of the players would learn how their partners had responded in each play of the game. (See chapter 2 for a description of how confidentiality was maintained.)

In one version of the experiment (the "unlimited" version), subjects were told that they could make promises not to defect, but they were also told that the anonymity of their responses would render such promises unenforceable. In two other versions of the experiment (the "intermediate" and "limited" versions), subjects were not permitted to make promises about their strategies. The latter two versions differed from one another in terms of the length of pregame interaction, with up to thirty

TABLE 9.1
Three Experimental Conditions

Experimental Condition	Pre-game meeting period	Permitted communication	Number of subjects
Unlimited	30 minutes	Complete freedom of communication, including freedom to make promises to cooperate	99
Intermediate	Up to 30 minutes	Promises not permitted; otherwise, complete freedom	84
Limited	Up to 10 minutes	Communication about the game not permitted; otherwise, complete freedom	84

minutes permitted for the intermediate groups and no more than ten minutes for the limited groups (see table 9.1).

Results for the Sample as a Whole

For the sample as a whole there were a total of 267 games, which means a total of 534 choices between cooperation and defection. The choices for economics majors and nonmajors are shown in figure 9.7, where we see that the defection rate for economics majors was 60.4 percent, as compared to only 38.8 percent for nonmajors.

Needless to say, this pattern of differences is strongly supportive of the hypothesis that economics majors are more likely than nonmajors to behave self-interestedly.[2]

Adding Control Variables

Earlier we noted that one possible explanation for the observed differences between economics students and others is that economics students are more likely than others to be male. Using ordinary least squares regression analysis, we estimated how defection rates varied by sex, age, and experimental condition.[3]

Consistent with a variety of other findings on sex differences in cooperation (see, for example, the studies cited in Gilligan [1982]), we estimated that the probability of a male defecting was almost .24 higher than the corresponding probability for a female. Even after controlling

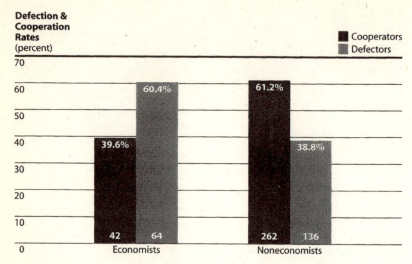

Figure 9.7 Defection and Cooperation Rates for the Sample as a Whole

for the influence of gender, we estimated that the probability of an economics major defecting is almost .17 higher than the corresponding probability for a nonmajor.

In the same regression study, the estimated defection rate was more than 9 percent greater for subjects in the intermediate category than for those in the unlimited category. The estimated defection rate for subjects in the limited category was almost 33 percent greater than for those in the unlimited category. Finally, we estimated that the overall defection rate declined at an average rate of almost 7 percent per year as students progressed through school. This pattern will prove important when we take up the question of whether training in economics is the cause of higher defection rates for economics majors.

The Unlimited Subsample

Focusing on subjects in the unlimited subsample, we see in figure 9.8 that the difference between economics majors and nonmajors virtually disappears once subjects are permitted to make promises to cooperate. For this subsample, the defection rate for economics majors is 28.6 percent, for nonmajors 25.9 percent.

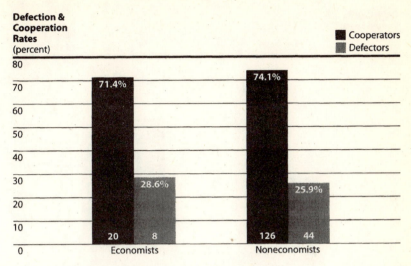

Figure 9.8 The Unlimited Subsample (Promises Permitted)

The Intermediate and Limited Subsamples

Because the higher defection rates for economics majors are largely attributable to the no-promises conditions of the experiment, the remainder of our analysis focuses on subjects in the limited and intermediate groups. The conditions encountered by these groups are of special significance because they come closest to approximating the conditions that characterize social dilemmas encountered in practice. After all, people rarely have an opportunity to look one another in the eye and promise not to litter on deserted beaches or disconnect the smog control devices on their cars.

Figure 9.9 portrays the choices for the pooled limited and intermediate groups. Comparing the entries in figure 9.9 with figure 9.8, we see clear evidence of the higher defection rates of both economics majors and nonmajors. The defection rates of 71.8 percent and 47.3 percent for economics majors and nonmajors, respectively, differ significantly from one another at the .01 level.

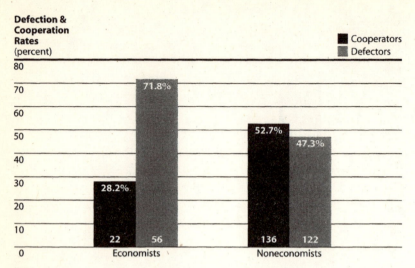

Figure 9.9 Defection and Cooperation Rates for the No-Promises Subsample

Reasons for Cooperation and Defection

As part of the exit questionnaire that tested our subjects' understanding of the payoffs associated with different combinations of choices, we also asked them to state their reasons for making the choices they did. We hypothesized that economists would be more inclined to construe the objective of the game in self-interested terms, and therefore more likely to refer exclusively to features of the game itself when describing reasons for their choices. By contrast, we expected the noneconomists to be more open to alternative ways of interpreting the game, and thus more likely to look to their partners for cues about how to play. Accordingly, we expected noneconomists to refer more often to their feelings about their partners, aspects of human nature, and so on. This is precisely the pattern we found. Among the sample of economics students, 31 percent made exclusive reference to features of the game itself in explaining their chosen strategies, as compared with only 17 percent of the non-economists. The probability of obtaining such divergent responses by chance is less than .05.

Another possible explanation for the economists' higher defection rates is that economists may be more likely than others to expect their partners to defect. The self-interest model, after all, encourages such an expectation, and we know from other experiments that most subjects defect if they are told that their partners are going to defect. To investigate the role of expectations, we asked students in an upper-division public finance course in Cornell's economics department whether they would cooperate or defect in a one-shot prisoner's dilemma if they knew *with certainty* that their partner was going to cooperate. Most of these students were economics majors in their junior and senior years. Of the 31 students returning our questionnaires, 18 (58 percent) reported that they would defect, while only 13 indicated that they would cooperate. By contrast, just 34 percent (14 of 41) noneconomics Cornell undergraduates who were given the same questionnaire reported that they would defect on a partner they knew would cooperate. For the same two groups of subjects, almost all respondents (30 of 31 economics students and 36 of 41 noneconomics students) said they would defect if they knew their partner would defect. From these responses, we conclude that while expectations of partner performance do indeed play a strong role in predicting behavior, defection rates would remain significantly higher for economists than for noneconomists even if both groups held identical expectations about partner performance.

Why Do Economists Behave Differently?

In the preceding sections we have seen evidence that economists behave less cooperatively than noneconomists along a variety of different dimensions. This difference in behavior might be exclusively the result of training in economics. Alternatively, it might exist simply because people who chose to major in economics were different initially. Or it might be some combination of these two effects. This section reports evidence suggesting that training in economics plays a causal role.

Comparing Upperclassmen and Underclassmen

If economics training plays a causal role in uncooperative behavior, then we would expect defection rates in the prisoner's dilemma experiments to rise with exposure to training in economics. Again focusing on the no-promises subsample, the defection rates are broken down by major and

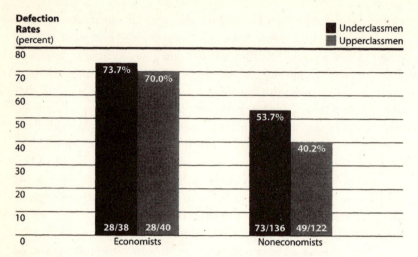

Figure 9.10 Defection Rates for Upper- and Underclassmen

level of education in figure 9.10. As shown, the defection rate for eco-nomics majors is virtually the same for both upperclassmen (juniors and seniors) and underclassmen (freshmen and sophomores). By contrast, the defection rate for nonmajors is approximately 33 percent higher for underclassmen than for upperclassmen.

The pattern shown in figure 9.10 continues to hold when we control for the effects of other sex and experimental condition using regression analysis.[4] Thus, we found that defection probabilities did not differ signif-icantly between upperclass economics majors and underclass economics majors. For nonmajors, defection probabilities were sharply lower than for majors in each category, and fell by more than .16 with the transition to upperclass status.

For students in general there is thus a pronounced tendency toward more cooperative behavior with movement toward graduation, a trend that is conspicuously absent for economics majors. On the basis of the available evidence, we are in no position to say whether the trend for noneconomists reflects something about the content of noneconomics courses. But regardless of the causes of this trend, the fact that it is not present for economists is consistent with the hypothesis that training in

economics plays at least some causal role in the lower observed cooperation rates of economists.

Honesty Surveys

In a further attempt to assess whether training in economics inhibits
cooperation in social dilemmas, we posed a pair of ethical dilemmas to
students in two introductory microeconomics courses at Cornell University and to a control group of students in an introductory astronomy
course, also at Cornell. In one dilemma, the owner of a small business is
shipped ten computers but is billed for only nine and the question is
whether the owner will inform the computer company of the error. Subjects are first asked to estimate the chances (0–100 percent) that the
owner would point out the mistake, and then, on the same response
scale, to indicate how likely *they* would be to point out the error if they
were the owner. The second dilemma concerns whether a lost envelope
containing $100 and bearing the owner's name and address is likely to
be returned by the person who finds it. Subjects are first asked to imagine that they have lost the envelope and to estimate the likelihood that a
stranger would return it. They are then asked to assume that the roles are
reversed and to indicate the chances that they would return the money
to a stranger.

Students in each class completed the questionnaire on two occasions,
first during the initial week of class in September, and then during the
final week of class in December. (The complete questionnaire is repro-
duced in the appendix, p. 179.)

For each of the four questions, each student was coded as being "more
honest" if the probability checked for that question rose between September and December; "less honest" if it fell during that period; and "no
change" if it remained the same. Our hypothesis was that even a single
semester of introductory microeconomics would have a measurable effect both on students' expectations of the level of self-interested behavior
in society and on their own propensities to behave self-interestedly.

The first introductory microeconomics instructor (instructor A) whose
students we surveyed was a mainstream economist with research interests
in industrial organization and game theory. In class lectures, this instruc-

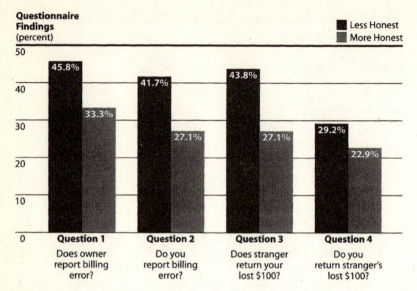

Figure 9.11 Questionnaire Findings: Introductory Microeconomics A

tor placed heavy emphasis on the prisoner's dilemma and related illustrations of how survival imperatives often militate against cooperation. The second microeconomics instructor (instructor B) was a specialist in economic development in Maoist China who did not emphasize such material to the same degree, but did assign a mainstream introductory text. On the basis of these differences, our expectation was that any observed effects of economics training should be stronger in instructor A's class than in instructor B's. The results for the three classes are summarized in figures 9.11–9.13. (The percentages for each question add up to 100 percent when the "no change" category is included.)

As figures 9.11 and 9.12 indicate, a tendency toward more cynical responses was observed in instructor A's introductory economics class but not in instructor B's. In our control group of introductory astronomy students (figure 9.13), there was a weak tendency toward less cynical expectations and behavior over the course of the semester.

It may seem natural to wonder whether the differences reflected in figures 9.11 and 9.12 might stem in part from the fact that students chose their instructors rather than being randomly assigned. Perhaps the

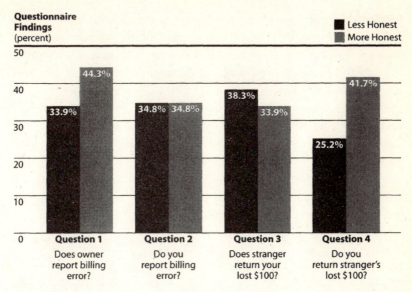

Figure 9.12 Questionnaire Findings: Introductory Microeconomics B

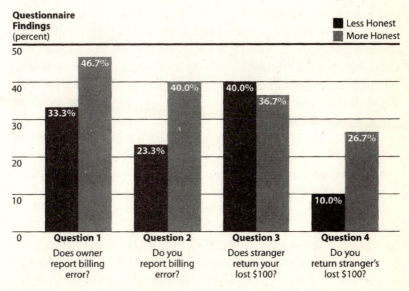

Figure 9.13 Questionnaire Findings: Introduction to Astronomy

ideological reputations of the two professors were known in advance to many students, with the result that a disproportionate number of the least cynical students chose to take instructor B's course. Two observations, however, weigh heavily against this interpretation. First, the average values of the initial responses to the four questions were in fact virtually the same for both classes.[5] And second, note that figures 9.11 and 9.12 record not the *level* of cynicism but the *change* in that level between the beginning and end of the course. Figure 9.12 thus tells us that even if the students in microeconomics A were more cynical to begin with, they became still more so during the course of the semester. This finding is consistent with the hypothesis that emphasis on the self-interest model tends to inhibit cooperation.

DISCUSSION

There have been several previous attempts to discover whether economists behave in more self-interested ways than do noneconomists. The Marwell and Ames finding of a greater tendency to free-ride on the part of economists is uncertain because their samples of economists and noneconomists were different on so many dimensions other than academic history and interests. The Carter and Irons findings on the ultimatum bargaining game were subject to an alternative interpretation based on the possibility that economics majors may have held different views on how performance in the preliminary word game affected entitlements in the ultimatum game.

We believe our prisoner's dilemma results constitute the clearest demonstration to date of a large difference in the extent to which economists and noneconomists behave self-interestedly. And our survey of charitable giving lends additional support to the hypothesis that economists are more likely than others to free-ride.

But we also emphasize that both of these exercises produced evidence that economists behave in traditionally communitarian ways under at least some circumstances. For example, they reported spending as much time as others in volunteer activities, and their total gifts to charity were only slightly less than would have been expected on the basis of their incomes. Finally, in the unlimited version of our prisoner's dilemma experiments, where subjects were allowed to promise to cooperate, economists were almost as likely to cooperate as noneconomists were.

We also found evidence consistent with the view that the differences in cooperativeness are caused in part by training in economics. First, we saw that the gap in defection rates between economics majors and nonmajors tends to widen as students move toward graduation. Second, we saw that introductory microeconomics, at least if taught in a certain way, seems to affect student attitudes toward honesty.

Clearly, our evidence for the existence of a difference between the behavior of economists and noneconomists is more compelling than our evidence for the causal role of economics training in creating that difference. But there is additional indirect evidence for such a role. One of the clearest patterns to emerge in several decades of experimental research on the prisoner's dilemma is that the behavior of any given player is strongly influenced by that player's prediction about what his partner will do (again, see the survey by Dawes [1980]). In experiments involving noneconomists, people who expect their partners to cooperate usually cooperate themselves, and those who expect their partners to defect almost always defect. In our experiments, economists were 42 percent more likely than noneconomists to predict that their partners would defect. It would be remarkable indeed if none of this difference in outlook were the result of repeated exposure to a behavioral model whose unequivocal prediction is that people will defect whenever self-interest dictates.

CONCLUDING REMARKS

For the sake of discussion, suppose that exposure to the self-interest model does, in fact, cause people to behave more selfishly. Should this be a cause for concern? To the extent that norms favoring cooperation help solve prisoner's dilemmas and other market failures, one cost of a rise in selfish behavior is a fall in the real value of economic output. Who bears this cost? By conventional accounts, it is those who continue to behave cooperatively — a troubling outcome on equity grounds. The evidence we saw in chapter 3 suggested, however, that the ultimate victims of noncooperative behavior may be the very people who practice it.

Suppose, for example, that some people always cooperate in one-shot prisoner's dilemmas while others always follow the seemingly dominant strategy of defecting. If people are free to interact with others of their own choosing, and if there are cues that distinguish cooperators from defectors, then cooperators will interact selectively with one another and earn higher payoffs than defectors. In chapter 2 we saw that even on the basis of brief encounters involving strangers, experimental subjects are adept at predicting who will cooperate and who will defect in prisoner's dilemma games. If people are even better at predicting the behavior of people they know well, it seems that the direct pursuit of material self-interest may indeed often be self-defeating.

These observations do not challenge the obvious importance of self-interest as a human motive. But they do suggest the need for a richer model of human behavior, one that explicitly recognizes that people who hold cooperative motives often come out ahead.

Appendix
Ethics Questionnaire

This questionnaire is part of an ongoing study of attitudes toward ethical issues that arise in business and personal life. Please read each question carefully and try to imagine yourself in the situation it describes. Then check the most appropriate response category for each question.

QUESTION #1.
In an effort to increase productivity, the owner of a small business has ordered ten personal computers for use by his staff. When the UPS shipment arrives, he notices that the invoice from the mail-order house bills for only nine PCs, even though all ten were included with the shipment.

The owner has two options. (1) He can inform the mail-order house of its error and ask to be billed for the correct amount; or (2) he can pay the amount shown on the invoice and take no further action.

If the owner pays the amount shown, the worst thing that can happen is that the mail-order house may later discover its error and bill him for the tenth computer. There is a high probability (.99, say) that the error will never be discovered.

What do you believe the chances are that the owner will inform the mail-order house of its mistake and ask to be billed for the correct amount? (Check one.)

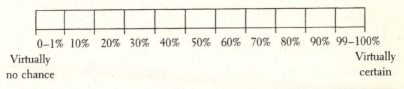

0–1% 10% 20% 30% 40% 50% 60% 70% 80% 90% 99–100%
Virtually   Virtually
no chance   certain

QUESTION #2.
If YOU were the owner in the situation described in Question #1, what are the chances you would inform the mail-order house of its mistake and ask to be billed for the correct amount? (Check one.)

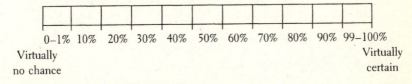

0–1% 10% 20% 30% 40% 50% 60% 70% 80% 90% 99–100%
Virtually   Virtually
no chance   certain

QUESTION #3.

After attending a football game, you return home to discover that you have lost an envelope from your jacket pocket. The envelope contains $100 in cash and has your name and address written on the outside. A stranger has found the envelope.

What would you say the chances are that this person will return your $100 to you? (Check one.)

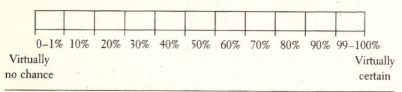

```
0–1%  10%  20%  30%  40%  50%  60%  70%  80%  90%  99–100%
```

Virtually   Virtually
no chance   certain

QUESTION #4.

If YOU found $100 in an envelope like the one described in Question #3, what are the chances that you would return the stranger's cash? (Check one.)

```
0–1%  10%  20%  30%  40%  50%  60%  70%  80%  90%  99–100%
```

Virtually   Virtually
no chance   certain

For each of the following, please check the category that applies to you:

Sex: male _____   female _____

Class: freshman _____   sophomore _____

        junior _____   senior _____ other _____

There will be a follow-up to this questionnaire in December. In order to match the follow-up questionnaire with this one, we need an identifying code for each of you, one that preserves your anonymity and that you will be able to recall easily in December. Past experience has taught that a code with these properties can be made from your middle name and your mother's maiden name.

Your middle name _____

Your mother's maiden name _____

Thank you very much for your cooperation.

NOTES

1. This allocation procedure is described in a longer, unpublished version of the Carter and Irons paper (1990).

2. Because each subject responded twice, the 534 choices reported in figure 9.7 are not statistically independent, and so the most direct test of statistical significance, the chi-square test, is inappropriate for the sample as a whole. To overcome this problem, we performed a chi-square test on the number of subjects who made the same choice — cooperate or defect — in *both* of their games. There were 207 such subjects (78 percent of the sample). The pattern of results observed in this restricted sample is essentially the same as the one observed for the sample as a whole.

3. Because each subject played the game twice, the individual responses are not statistically independent. To get around this problem, we limited our sample to the 207 subjects who either cooperated with, or defected on, each of their two partners. The sixty subjects who cooperated with one partner and defected on the other were deleted from the sample. The dependent variable is the subject's choice of strategy, coded as 0 for "cooperate" and 1 for "defect." The independent variables are "econ," which takes the value 1 for economics majors, 0 for all others; "unlimited," which is 1 for subjects in the unlimited version of the experiment, 0 for all others; "intermediate," which is 1 for subjects in the intermediate version, 0 for all others; "limited," which is the reference category; "sex," coded as 1 for males, 0 for females; and "class," coded as 1 for freshmen, 2 for sophomores, 3 for juniors, and 4 for seniors.

The Effect of Education Level on Defection Rates

Dependent variable: own response				
Source	Sum of Squares	df	Mean Square	F-ratio
Regression	11.1426	5	2.229	11.5
Residual	38.9540	201	.193801	

Variable	Coefficient	s.e.	t-ratio
Constant	.579127	.1041	5.57
econ	.168835	.0780	2.16
unlimited	.00	—	—
intermediate	−.091189	.0806	−1.13
limited	−.329572	.0728	−4.53
sex	.239944	.0642	3.74
class	−.065363	.0303	−2.16

$R^2 = 22.2\%$ R^2(adjusted) $= 20.3\%$
$s = 0.4402$ with $207 - 6 = 201$ degrees of freedom

Because the conventional assumptions regarding the distribution of the error term are not satisfied in the case of linear models with dichotomous dependent variables, the standard OLS significance tests are not valid. So we also ran models based on the probit and logit transformations. The statistical significance patterns shown by the coefficients from these transformed models were the same as for the OLS model. Because the coefficients of the OLS model are more easily interpreted, we report the remainder of our results in that format only.

4. As did the whole-sample regression reported earlier, the regression reported below employs only those subjects who either cooperated in both games or defected in both games.

Dependent variable: own response

Source	Sum of Squares	df	Mean Square	F-ratio
Regression	5.03599	5	1.0072	4.61
Residual	25.7624	118	.218325	

Variable	Coefficient	s.e.	t-ratio
Constant	.628734	.1436	4.38
Limited	.00	—	—
intermediate	−.095040	.0876	−1.09
sex	.257538	.0896	2.88
econ 1,2	.00	—	—
econ 3,4	−.026936	.1623	−.166
nonecon 1,2	−.151050	.1426	−1.06
nonecon 3,4	−.313266	.1427	−2.20

$R^2 = 16.4\%$ R^2(adjusted) = 12.8%
$s = 0.4673$ with $124 - 6 = 118$ degrees of freedom

5. For microeconomics A, the average September responses to questions 1–4 were 30.9, 50, 30.4, and 70.1, respectively; for microeconomics B, the corresponding responses were 29.9, 47.4, 34.4, and 68.2.

Epilogue
The Importance of Sanctions

ALTHOUGH THE ESSAYS in this volume take issue with many elements of the received wisdom of neoclassical economics, it would be a mistake to read them as hostile to the economic way of thinking. Indeed, among the growing number of economists working at the intersections of economics and other disciplines in recent years, I come closer than most to embracing the rational choice tradition of neoclassical economics. For the most part I assume that people have reasonably well-defined goals and try to achieve them as best they can.

Sometimes I emphasize that this effort is crude and approximate, as in chapter 7 when I discussed how cognitive limitations seem to affect patterns of charitable giving. But my main departure from the dominant neoclassical tradition is that the goals I attribute to people are much broader than the ones generally assumed.

Many feel uncomfortable about broadening the model in this way, rightly fearing that having the latitude to insert new tastes on an ad hoc basis would rob it of its explanatory power. But I have argued that this concern fades if we have principled criteria for deciding which tastes can be added. Under the adaptive rationality standard proposed in chapter 3, a new taste can be added if two conditions are met. First we must offer evidence that a significant fraction of the population actually holds the taste in question. And second we must offer a plausible account as to why holding that taste need not handicap efforts to acquire resources in competitive environments.

The first condition is easily satisfied for many components of motivation that transcend narrow self-interest. For example, close observers of human behavior have never seriously questioned that emotions such as sympathy, guilt, anger, and envy are widespread. But because these emotions often motivate people to incur avoidable costs, the second criterion of the adaptive rationality standard is clearly more problematic. Sympathy for one's trading partner, for example, has been shown to make people trustworthy even when they could have earned far more by cheating. Anger about having been treated unjustly often leads people to pursue costly retaliation, even when that will not undo the original injury. Caring about relative payoffs often leads people to reject one-sided offers, even when their wealth would have been increased by accepting them. And strong emotional bonds of love often lead people to remain with their partners even when new opportunities arise that are objectively more valuable.

But although emotions often lead us to incur avoidable costs, they can also generate important material benefits. If potential employers can identify you as trustworthy, you immediately become a more attractive candidate for positions that entail temptations to cheat. If potential aggressors can identify you as someone who cares strongly about justice, you can credibly threaten to retaliate even when the costs of retaliation would exceed the material benefits. And if you are known to care about relative payoffs in addition to absolute payoffs, you are likely to be a much more effective bargainer.

Does broadening the traditional neoclassical model's portrayal of human motivation in these ways challenge any important core beliefs held by economists? More specifically, do the amendments supported by the adaptive rationality standard challenge the economics profession's faith in the celebrated invisible hand, which holds that unregulated market forces translate the behavior of selfish individuals into beneficial outcomes for society as a whole? Some elements of the broader motivational repertoire I propose render the invisible hand considerably less powerful than most economists would like to believe. Yet there are other elements that render the invisible hand far more effective than even the most ardent free-market proponent might have dared hope. I will consider examples of each type in turn.

First an example of a specific taste that undercuts the invisible hand: All economists recognize that the invisible hand breaks down when the self-serving actions of one individual inflict unintended but harmful side-effects on others. Environmental pollution is the most commonly cited example, but the problem is really far more general. Although standard neoclassical models assume that absolute consumption is the only important determinant of individual well-being, for example, I described evidence in chapters 6 and 8 suggesting that relative consumption is even more important. The basic idea is that we aren't born with an absolute scale for evaluating many of the goods and services that constitute our standard of living. Rather, our evaluations depend inescapably on context. In the economist Richard Layard's famous line, "In a poor country a man can show his wife he loves her by giving her a rose, but in a rich country he must give a dozen roses."

If context shapes our evaluation of a specific good, virtually every spending decision regarding that good inflicts harmful side-effects on others by altering the relevant context. Thus, if some people in a given reference group begin giving larger bouquets, for whatever reason, the frame of reference then shifts in a way that makes any given bouquet less effective for its intended purpose than before. This effect is formally equivalent to the damage caused by actions that cause environmental pollution. Under the circumstances, there can be no general presumption that an invisible hand will translate selfish individual actions into the best possible social outcome. On the contrary, wasteful positional arms races will be the norm.

By contrast, other specific tastes that meet the criteria imposed by the adaptive rationality standard actually serve to enhance the efficacy of the invisible hand. Consider again the example of environmental pollution. When negotiation among the relevant parties is impractical, standard models predict an inefficiently high level of environmental pollution in unregulated markets. This prediction is used to justify laws and regulations aimed at curtailing pollution.

But there are clear limits to the law's ability to regulate human behavior. If someone wants to pour a gallon of unwanted pesticide down his basement drain, for example, there is no practical way to apprehend and punish him. Fortunately, the law is not our only tool for addressing the conflict between self-interest and the common good. We can also rely on moral suasion. Do you know someone you feel sure would return a gallon of unwanted pesticide to a government disposal center a half hour's drive away, rather than simply pour it down her basement drain, even though the latter action would be far more convenient and would entail no significant personal harmful effects? If so then you accept not only that some people are driven by pro-social motives, but also that the presence of such motives can be reliably discerned by outsiders in at least some cases. When these conditions are met, the adaptive rationality standard calls our attention to the fact that environmental damage can be avoided in many cases for which traditional neoclassical models insist it is inevitable.

The mere possibility of spontaneous, self-sustaining moral behavior is a profoundly optimistic notion. But we must be careful not to become intoxicated by it. In particular, it provides no reason whatever to just sit back and allow events to unfold. For example, the fact that some individuals and corporations may pollute less than the law permits is no reason to think we would be better off to relegate air and water quality standards to the invisible hand of the market.

Not all policy makers appear to have grasped this lesson. From his approach to pollution abatement as Texas governor to his approach to corporate malfeasance as president, George W. Bush's watchword has been voluntary compliance. Explaining his initial opposition to the strict criminal sanctions in the corporate fraud legislation enacted in the summer of 2002, for example, he conceded that although tougher laws might help, "ultimately, the ethics of American business depend on the conscience of America's business leaders."

Although it is surely a positive step for public officials to try to nurture our inclination to do the right thing, there is also a downside to such heavy emphasis on voluntary compliance. It overlooks the critical role that enforcement measures have always played in society's efforts to curb narrow self-interest for the common good. Without such measures, we must ask those who comply voluntarily to shoulder an unfair burden.

The nature of the problem is vividly illustrated by a waiter's decision about whether to report his earnings from tips to the IRS. According to a 1991 estimate, 84 percent of such earnings went unreported at tax time. That figure is not a sign that waiters are less honest than others. Rather, it is a simple reflection of the fact that waiters were paid artificially low wages precisely because their earnings from tips were so difficult for the IRS to monitor.

To see why, consider a waiter whose alternative to waiting tables is an equally attractive salaried job at $200 a day, all of it taxable at a rate of 20 percent, for a net take-home pay of $160 a day. If waiters could earn $140 dollars a day in tips, and if tips could be easily monitored and taxed at the same 20 percent rate, restaurateurs would have to pay an additional $60 a day in salary in order to attract applicants for their positions. But if failure to declare tips carries no risk of penalty, a waiter could pay only the $12 tax bill on his $60 daily salary, leaving him with a daily net take-home pay of $188, or $28 more than his after-tax pay in a fully salaried, fully taxed position.

The upshot is that restaurateurs can still attract plenty of waiters even if they pay considerably less than $60 a day. How much less? If there were many people holding salaried positions who would be willing to wait tables if they could make more money (a reasonable assumption), a restaurateur could pay, say, $30 a day, in which case a waiter who didn't declare his tips would still end up with $4 a day more in take-home pay than in a salaried position.

Notice, however, that at that salary, a waiter who declared all of his $160 in tips (thus paying an extra $32 a day in taxes) would take home $28 a day *less* than if he worked in the salaried job. It is one thing to ask people to forgo ill-gotten gains, but it is quite another to demand that they accept less than a fair market wage. Under the circumstances, it seems not only quixotic to expect waiters to declare tips to the IRS, but also unfair.

If we want waiters to pay taxes on their tips, we must come up with a way to make it in their interest to report them. In 1995 the IRS acknowledged the futility of a pure voluntary compliance strategy by launching its Tip Reporting Alternative Commitment Program, under which restaurateurs and other similar employers face stiff sanctions if they do not "comply with tip reporting and payment obligations, maintain current records, and establish procedures for employees to accurately report tips." Under this program, tip income reported to the IRS reached $7 billion by 1998, up from $3.9 billion in 1993. And as the share of tips that are effectively taxed has risen, competition has forced restaurateurs to compensate by paying higher salaries to waiters.

The futility of exclusive reliance on voluntary compliance is further illustrated by the forces confronting honest executives as they weigh how to report their company's earnings. They know that many entries in the company's financial statements necessarily entail subjective judgments. Some, for instance, hinge on estimates and assumptions about the future, others on imperfect models for imputing monetary values to non-market assets. For any firm, there is thus a broad range of earnings estimates that could be defended as reasonable.

Therein lies the problem, because a company's ability to finance its future growth depends strongly on how its current reported earnings compare with those of rival firms. After all, it is on this basis that capital markets infer which firms are most likely to succeed. Stock prices often fall sharply in the short run for those reporting relatively low current earnings, increasing their risk of failure in the long run. Under the circumstances, it is difficult to see how even the most scrupulous executives could justify calculating their company's earnings on the basis of strictly neutral, let alone pessimistic, assumptions. On the plausible forecast that most other companies will report earnings near the optimistic end of the reasonable range, failure to do likewise would be to understate the company's true prospects.

Worse still, this situation is unstable, because the standards that define acceptable accounting judgments are inherently dependent on context. When almost all companies issue optimistic earnings reports, such reports come to be viewed as normal. Even the most cautious executives then feel pressure to report their earnings more aggressively, creating room for their more aggressive counterparts to push the envelope still further.

Given this dynamic and the enormous sums at stake in the battle for corporate survival, careful monitoring and stiff sanctions against violators are essential. It is one thing to ask people to forgo ill-gotten gains but quite another to ask them to commit economic suicide. Many of World-Com's competitors were injured, some even driven into bankruptcy, by their failure to match WorldCom's aggressive accounting practices (and WorldCom itself would still be flying high except for the sudden collapse of revenue in the telecommunications industry).

Essentially the same logic applies to all other forms of malfeasance in the marketplace. If athletes can gain ground at the expense of their rivals by taking steroids without penalty, many will do so. And if people can claim questionable tax exemptions without penalty, many will do so. These actions pressure others to respond in kind, which in turn shifts the standards that define acceptable conduct.

If we want people to restrain themselves for the common good, the sacrifices we demand must be equitable. To ask athletes not to use steroids in the absence of effective sanctions, however, is to penalize those who comply while rewarding those who don't. To ask people to be scrupulous in their tax filings in an audit-free environment is to reduce the effective tax rate for dishonest taxpayers while increasing it for honest ones.

Congress was wise to include criminal sanctions in its corporate fraud legislation of 2002. Major League Baseball would be wise to revise the steroid ban in its 2002 labor agreement to include frequent random testing and stiff penalties against violators. And President Bush might want to rethink the wisdom of the sharp IRS staff and budget cuts that have reduced the tax audit rate by more than half since 1996.

As Adam Smith himself was well aware, the invisible hand of the marketplace does not always produce the greatest good for all. When individual and social interests conflict, calls for voluntary compliance must be supplemented by sanctions that are potent enough to matter. As President Reagan aptly put it, "Trust, but verify."

References

Abegglen, James. 1973. *Management and Worker*. Tokyo: Sophia University.

Ainslie, George. 1992. *Picoeconomics*. New York: Cambridge University Press.

Akerlof, George. 1970. "The Market for Lemons." *Quarterly Journal of Economics* 84: 488–500.

Akerlof, George A., and Yellen, Janet L. 1990. "The Fair Wage-Effort Hypothesis and Unemployment." *Quarterly Journal of Economics* 105: 255–83.

———. 1983. "Loyalty Filters." *The American Economic Review* 73 (March): 54–63.

Andreoni, James. 1986. "Private Giving to Public Goods: The Limits to Altruism." University of Michigan Department of Economics Working Paper.

Argyle, Scott T., and Janet Dean. 1965. "Eye Contact, Distance, and Affiliation." *Sociometry* 28: 289–304.

Ashenfelter, Orley, and J. Mooney. 1968. "Graduate Education, Ability, and Earnings." *Review of Economics and Statistics* 50, no. 1 (Feb.).

Axelrod, Robert. 1984. *The Evolution of Cooperation*. New York: Basic Books.

Axelrod, Robert, and William Hamilton. 1981. "The Evolution of Cooperation." *Science* 211: 1390–96.

Banfield, Edward. 1958. *The Moral Basis of a Backward Society*. Glencoe, Ill.: Free Press.

Bargh, John A. "The Automaticity of Everyday Life." *Advances in Social Cognition* 10: 1–61.

Baumhart, Raymond. 1968. *Ethics in Business*. New York: Holt, Rinehart, and Winston.

Bavelas, J. B., A. Black, C. R. Lemery, and J. Mullett. 1986. "I *Show* How You Feel: Motor Mimicry as a Communicative Act." *Journal of Personality and Social Psychology* 50: 322–29.

Bazerman, Max. 1993. Personal conversation.

Belcher, David W., and Thomas J. Atchison. 1987. *Compensation Administration*. 2d ed. Englewood Cliffs: Prentice Hall.

Brockner, J., and W. C. Swap. 1976. "Effects of Repeated Exposure and Attitudinal Similarity on Self-Disclosure and Interpersonal Attraction." *Journal of Personality and Social Psychology* 33: 531–40.

Bruell, Jan. 1970. "Heritability of Emotional Behavior." In *Physiological Correlates of Emotion*, edited by Perry Black. New York: Academic Press.

Business Week. 1967. "Should Paid Witnesses Say So?" 9 September, 9.

Cacioppo, John T., Joseph R. Priester, and Gary G. Berntson. 1993. "Rudimentary Determinants of Attitudes, II: Arm Flexion and Extension Have Differential Effects on Attitudes." *Journal of Personality and Social Psychology* 65: 5–17.

Carr, Albert. [1968] 1993. "Is Business Bluffing Ethical?" *Harvard Business Review*, Jan./Feb. 1968. Reprinted in Thomas Donaldson and Patricia Werhane, eds. *Ethical Issues in Business*, 4th ed., 90–97. Englewood Cliffs, N.J.

Carter, John, and Michael Irons. 1990. "Are Economists Different, and If So, Why?" College of the Holy Cross (longer, unpublished version of the paper below).

———. 1991. "Are Economists Different, and If So, Why?" *Journal of Economic Perspectives* 5 (Spring).

Cellucci, Anthony, and David DeVries. 1978. *Measuring Managerial Satisfaction: A Manual for the MJSQ, Technical Report II*. Center for Creative Literature.

Chapman, Graham. 1989. *The Complete Monty Python's Flying Circus: All the Words*. New York: Pantheon.

Chartrand, Tanya L., and John A. Bargh. 1998. "The Chameleon Effect: How the Perception-Behavior Link Facilitates Social Interaction." New York University. Mimeo.

Coleman, James S. 1990. *Foundations of Social Theory*. Cambridge, Mass.: Harvard University Press.

Congleton, Roger. 1980. "Competitive Process, Competitive Waste, and Institutions." In J. Buchanan, R. Tollison, and G. Tullock, eds. *Toward a Theory of the Rent-Seeking Society*, 153–79. College Station, Tex.: Texas A&M University Press.

Darwin, Charles. [1872] 1965. *The Expression of Emotions in Man and Animals*. Chicago: University of Chicago Press.

Dawes, Robyn. 1980. "Social Dilemmas." *Annual Review of Psychology* 31: 69–93.

Dawes, Robyn, Jeanne McTavish, and Harriet Shaklee. 1977. "Behavior, Communication, and Assumptions about Other people's Behavior in a Commons Dilemma Situation." *Journal of Personality and Social Psychology* 35: 1–11.

Dawkins, Richard. 1976. *The Selfish Gene*. New York: Oxford University Press.

Eagly, A. H., R. D. Ashmore, M. G. Makhijani, and L. C. Longo. 1991. "What Is Beautiful is Good, But . . . : A Meta-Analytic Review of Research on the Physical Attractiveness Stereotype." *Psychological Bulletin* 110: 109–28.

Ekman, Paul. 1985. *Telling Lies*. New York: Norton.

Elder, G. H., and E. C. Clipp. 1988. "Wartime Losses and Social Bonding: Influence across 40 Years in Men's Lives." *Psychiatry* 51: 177–98.

Etzioni, Amitai. 1988. *The Moral Dimension: Toward a New Economics*. New York: Free Press.

Frank, Robert H. 1984. "Are Workers Paid Their Marginal Products?" *American Economic Review* 74 (Sept.): 549–71.

———. 1985. *Choosing the Right Pond*. New York: Oxford University Press.

———. 1987. "If *Homo Economicus* Could Choose His Own Utility Function, Would He Want One with a Conscience?" *American Economic Review* 77 (Sept.): 593–604.

———. 1988. *Passions Within Reason.* New York: W. W. Norton.

———. 1992. "Melding Sociology and Economics: James Coleman's *Foundations of Social Theory.*" *Journal of Economic Literature* 30 (March): 147–70.

———. 1993. "Local Status, Fairness, and Wage Compression Revisited." Paper presented to Conference on the Economics and Psychology of Happiness and Fairness, London School of Economics, November.

———. 1996a. "What Price the Moral High Ground?" *Southern Economic Journal* July: 1–17.

———. 1996b. "Motivation, Cognition, and Charitable Giving." In *Giving,* edited by Jerome Schneewind, 130–52. Bloomington: Indiana University Press.

———. 1996c. "Can Socially Responsible Firms Survive in a Competitive Environment?" In David Messick and Ann Tenbrunsel, eds. *Codes of Conduct: Behavioral Research into Business Ethics.* 86–103. New York: Russell Sage.

———. 1998. "Social Norms as Positional Arms Control Agreements." In Louis Putterman and Avner Ben Ner, eds. *Values, Economics, and Organization,* 275–95. New York: Cambridge University Press.

———. 1999. *Luxury Fever.* New York: The Free Press.

———. 2002a. "Cooperation through Emotional Commitment." In Randolph Nesse, ed., *Evolution and the Capacity for Commitment.* 57–76. New York: Russell Sage.

———. 2002b. "Adaptive Rationality and the Moral Emotions." In Davidson, R. J., K. R. Scherer, and H. H. Goldsmith, eds. *Handbook of Affective Sciences.* New York: Oxford University Press.

———. 2003. "Introducing Moral Emotions Into Models of Rational Choice." In A.S.R. Manstead, N. H. Frijda, and A. H. Fischer, eds. *Feelings and Emotions: The Amsterdam Symposium.* New York: Cambridge University Press.

Frank, Robert H., and Philip J. Cook. 1993. "Winner-Take-All Markets." Unpublished manuscript. Cornell University.

———. 1995. *The Winner-Take-All Society.* New York: Free Press.

Frank, Robert H., Thomas Gilovich, and Dennis Regan. 1993a. "Does Studying Economics Inhibit Cooperation?" *Journal of Economic Perspectives* 7 (Spring): 159–71.

———. 1993b. "The Evolution of One-Shot Cooperation." *Ethology and Sociobiology* 14 (July): 247–56.

———. 1996. "Do Economists Make Bad Citizens?" *Journal of Economic Perspectives?* Spring.

Freeman, Richard B. 1993. "Me Give to Charity? Well, Since You Ask." Paper delivered at the Conference on the Economics and Psychology of Happiness and Fairness, London School of Economics, November.

Frey, Bruno and Alois Stutzer. *Happiness and Economics*, Princeton, NJ: Princeton University Press, 2002.

Friedman, Milton. 1970. "The Social Responsibility of Business is to Increase Its Profits." *New York Times Magazine*, 13 September.

Gardin, Hershel, Kalman J. Kaplan, Ira J. Firestone, and Gloria A. Cowan. 1973. "Proxemic Effects on Cooperation, Attitude, and Approach-Avoidance in a Prisoner's Dilemma Game." *Journal of Personality and Social Psychology* 27: 13–18.

Gauthier, David. 1985. *Morals by Agreement*. Oxford: Clarendon.

Gibbard, Alan. 1990. *Wise Choices, Apt Feelings: A Theory of Normative Judgment*. Cambridge, Mass.: Harvard University Press; Oxford: Oxford University Press.

Gilligan, Carol. 1982. *In a Different Voice*. Cambridge, Mass.: Harvard University Press.

Gilovich, Thomas. 1991. *How We Know What Isn't So*. New York: Free Press.

Glazer, Amihai, and Kai Konrad. 1992. "A Signalling Explanation for Private Charity." University of California, Irvine, Department of Economics Working Paper.

Gould, Stephen Jay. 1977. *Ever Since Darwin*. New York: W. W. Norton.

Granovetter, Mark. 1973. "The Strength of Weak Ties." *American Journal of Sociology* 77: 1360–80.

———. 1985. "Economic Action and Social Structure: The Problem of Embeddedness." *American Journal of Sociology* 91: 481–510.

Guth, Werner, Rolf Schmittberger, and Bernd Schwarze. 1982. "An Experimental Analysis of Ultimatum Bargaining." *Journal of Economic Behavior and Organization* 3: 367–88.

Hall, Edward T. 1982. *The Hidden Dimension*. New York: Anchor Books.

Handy, F., and E. Katz. 1998. "The Wage Differential between Nonprofit Institutions and Corporations: Getting More by Paying Less?" *Journal of Comparative Economics* 26, 2: 246–61.

Hatfield, Elaine, John T. Cacioppo, and Richard Rapson. 1994. *Emotional Contagion*. Paris: Cambridge University Press.

Hauser, Robert, and Thomas Daymont. 1977. "Schooling, Ability, and Earnings: Cross-Sectional Findings 8 to 14 Years After High School Graduation." *Sociology of Education* 50, no. 2 (July). 182–206.

Heimer, Mel. 1969. *The Long Count*. New York: Athenium.

Helson, Harry. 1964. *Adaptation Level Theory*. New York: Harper and Row.

Hirshleifer, Jack. 1987. "On the Emotions as Guarantors of Threats and Promises." In John Dupre, ed. *The Latest and the Best: Essays on Evolution and Optimality*. Cambridge, Mass.: The MIT Press.

Hume, David. [1740] 1978. *A Treatise of Human Nature*. Oxford: Oxford University Press.

Kahneman, Daniel, Jack Knetsch, and Richard Thaler. 1986a. "Fairness and the Assumptions of Economics." *Journal of Business* 59: S285–S300.

———. 1986b. "Perceptions of Unfairness: Constraints on Wealth Seeking." *American Economic Review* 76 (Sept.): 728–41.

Kiernan, V. G. 1988. *The Duel in European History: Honour and the Reign of Aristocracy*. New York: Oxford University Press.

Klein, Benjamin, and Keith Leffler. 1981. "The Role of Market Forces in Assuring Contractual Performance." *Journal of Political Economy* 89 (Aug.): 615–41.

Konrad, Alison, and Jeffrey Pfeffer. 1990. "Do You Get What You Deserve? Factors Affecting the Relationship between Productivity and Pay." *Administrative Science Quarterly* 35: 258–85.

Kuhn, Thomas. 1996. *The Structure of Scientific Revolutions*. 3d ed. Chicago: University of Chicago Press.

Lazarsfeld, Paul F., and Robert K. Merton. 1954. "Friendship as a Social Process." In *Freedom and Control in Modern Society*, edited by M. Berger. 18–66. Princeton: Van Nostrand.

Levine, David I. 1991. "Cohesiveness, Productivity, and Wage Dispersion." *Journal of Economic Behavior and Organization* 15: 237–55.

Lewin, K. 1935. *A Dynamic Theory of Personality*. New York: McGraw-Hill.

Lichtenstein, Sarah, Baruch Fischoff, and Lawrence Phillips. 1982. "Calibration of Probabilities: The State of the Art to 1980." In Daniel Kahneman, Paul Slovic, and Amos Tversky, eds., *Judgment Under Uncertainty: Heuristics and Biases*. 306–34. Cambridge: Cambridge University Press.

Linden, Paula S., Gail G. Penshel, and Jamienne S. Studley. 1989. "What Happened to the Class of '87?" *National Law Journal*, 27 March.

Lorenz, Edward. 1988. "Neither Friends Nor Strangers: Informal Networks of Subcontracting in French Industry." In Diego Gambetta, *Trust: The Making and Breaking of Cooperative Relations*. 194–210. New York: Basil Blackwell.

Loury, Glen. 1979. "Market Structure and Innovation." *Quarterly Journal of Economics*. August: 395–410.

Mangum, Garth L. 1964. *Wage Incentive Systems*. Berkeley: Institute of Industrial Relations, University of California.

Mansbridge, Jane J. 1990. *Beyond Self-Interest*. Chicago: University of Chicago Press.

Marwell, Gerald, and Ruth Ames. 1981. "Economists Free Ride, Does Anyone Else?" *Journal of Public Economics* 15: 295–310.

McClennen, Edward F. 1990. *Rationality and Dynamic Choice: Foundational Explorations*. New York: Cambridge University Press.

McGuire, Michael, M. Raleigh, and G. Brammer. 1982. "Sociopharmacology." *Annual Review of Pharmacological Toxicology* 22: 643–61.

Mervis, P. H., and Hackett, E. J. 1983. "Work and Workforce Characteristics in the Nonprofit Sector." *Monthly Labor Review*, April 3–12.

Miller, Lynn. 1987. "Debt Trap." *Student Lawyer*, 16 September 1987, 22–29.

Murstein, B. I., M. Cerreto, and M. MacDonald. 1977. "A Theory and Investigation of the Effect of Exchange-Orientation on Marriage and Friendship." *Journal of Marriage and the Family* 39: 543–48.

National Industrial Conference Board. 1970. "Incentive Plans for Salesmen." *Studies in Personnel Policy*, 217: 75–86.

Nye, Peter. 1993. "Mental Accounting and The Sunk Cost Effect: A Field Experiment." Paper presented at the Annual Meetings of the Association for Consumer Research, October.

Parfit, Derek. 1984. *Reasons and Persons*. Oxford: The Clarendon Press.

Patterson, Miles L. 1973. "Compensation in Nonverbal Immediacy Behaviors: A Review." *Sociometry* 36: 237–52.

Podolny, Joel. 1993. "A Status-Based Model of Market Competition." *American Journal of Sociology* 98 (Jan.): 829–72.

Preston, Anne E. "The Nonprofit Worker in a For-Profit World." *Journal of Labor Economics* 7, no. 4: 438–63.

Putnam, Robert. 2000. *Bowling Alone*. New York: Simon & Schuster.

Raleigh, Michael J., and Michael T. McGuire. 1994. "Serotonin, Aggression, and Violence in Vervet Monkeys." In *The Neurotransmitter Revolution: Serotonin, Social Behaivor, and the Law*, ed. by Roger Masters and Michael McGuire, 146–58. Carbondale: Southern Illinois University Press.

Rapoport, Anatol, and A. Chammah. 1965. *Prisoner's Dilemma*. Ann Arbor: University of Michigan Press.

Romer, David. 1992. "Why Do Firms Prefer More Able Workers?" University of California, Berkeley. Department of Economics. Mimeo.

Rosenberg, Morris. 1957. *Occupations and Values*. Glencoe, Ill.: Free Press.

Rothschild, Michael, and Joseph Stiglitz. 1976. "Equilibrium in Competitive Insurance Markets." *Quarterly Journal of Economics* 80: 629–49.

Sally, David. 1995. "Conversation and Cooperation in Social Dilemmas: A Meta-Analysis of Experiments from 1958 to 1972." *Rationality and Society* 7: 58–92.

———. 2000. "A General Theory of Sympathy, Mind-Reading, and Social Interaction, with an Application to the Prisoners' Dilemma." *Social Science Information* 39, no. 4: 567–634.

Schelling, Thomas C. 1960. *The Strategy of Conflict*. New York: Oxford University Press.

———. 1978a. "Altruism, Meanness, and other Potentially Strategic Behaviors." *American Economic Review* 68: 229–30.

———. 1978b. *Micromotives and Macrobehavior*. New York: W. W. Norton.

———. 1984. *Choice and Consequence*. Cambridge, Mass.: Harvard University Press.

Sen, Amartya. 1985. "Goals, Commitment, and Identity." *Journal of Law, Economics, and Organization* 1: 341–55.

Shackett, J., and J. M. Trapani. "Earnings Differentials and Market Structure." *The Journal of Human Resources* 12, no. 4: 518–31.

Sharp, L. M. 1970. *Education and Employment: The Early Years of College Graduates.* Baltimore: Johns Hopkins University Press.

Skyrms, Brian. 1998. "Mutual Aid: Darwin Meets the Logic of Decision." In Peter Danielson, ed. *Modeling Rationality, Morality, and Evolution* 379–407. New York: Oxford University Press.

Smith, Adam. [1759] 1966. *The Theory of Moral Sentiments.* New York: Kelley.

Solomon, Robert. 2003. *Not Passion's Slave: Emotions and Choice.* New York: Oxford University Press.

Strack, Fritz, L. L. Martin, and S. Stepper. 1988. "Inhibiting and Facilitating Conditions of the Human Smile: A Nonobtrusive Test of the Facial Feedback Hypothesis." *Journal of Personality and Social Psychology* 54: 768–76.

Studley, Jamienne S. 1989. "Financial Sacrifice Outside the Private Sector." *National Law Journal* 27 March.

Thaler, Richard H. 1980. "Toward a Positive Theory of Consumer Choice." *Journal of Economic Behavior and Organization*: 39–60.

———. 1985. "Mental Accounting and Consumer Choice." *Marketing Science* 4.

Tinbergen, Niko. 1952. "Derived Activities: Their Causation, Biological Significance, and Emancipation During Evolution." *Quarterly Review of Biology* 27: 1–32.

Trivers, Robert L. 1971. "The Evolution of Reciprocal Altruism." *Quarterly Review of Biology* 46: 35–57.

Tullock, Gordon. 1976. *The Vote Motive.* London: Institute for Economic Affairs.

Tversky, Amos, and Daniel Kahneman. 1981. "The Framing of Decisions and the Psychology of Choice" *Science* 211: 453–58.

Valley, Kathleen L., Joseph Moag, and Max H. Bazerman. 1998. "A Matter of Trust: Effects of Communication on the Efficiency and Distribution of Outcomes." *Journal of Economic Behavior and Organization* 34: 211–38.

Vitell, Scott J. and D. L. Davis. 1990. "The Relationship Between Ethics and Job Satisfaction: An Empirical Investigation." *Journal of Business Ethics* 9: 489–94.

Weisbrod, Burton. 1983. "Nonprofit and Proprietary Sector Behaviour: Wage Differentials Among Lawyers." *Journal of Labor Economics*, 1: 246–63.

Whyte, William F. 1955. *Money and Motivation.* New York: Harper and Brothers.

Wilkinson, F. 1979. *The Illustrated Book of Pistols.* London: Hamlyn.

Windsor, Robert, and Daniel Dumitru. 1988. "Anabolic Steroid Use by Athletes: How Serious Are the Health Hazards?" *Postgraduate Medicine*, 84.

Wright, Robert. 1994. *The Moral Animal.* New York: Pantheon.

Yezer, Anthony, Robert Goldfarb, and Paul Poppen. 1996. "Does Studying Economics Discourage Cooperation? Watch What We Do, Not What We Say." *Journal of Econonic Perspectives,* Spring.

Zajonc, Robert B., Pamela K. Adelmann, Shiela T. Murphy, and Paula M. Niedenthal. 1987. "Convergence in the Physical Appearance of Spouses." *Motivation and Emotion* 11: 335–46.

Index

accounting standards, vii, 187–88
adaptive rationality, 47–49, 57; consequentialist moral theory and, 54–56; an ecological model of, 49–51; human nature, image of, 54, 111; the invisible hand and, 184–85; literature related to, 51–52; local status and, 98; new tastes, conditions for adding based on, 183–84; voodoo causation and, 52–53
Ainslie, George, 23
Akerlof, George, 52, 63
altruism, 112–13, 119–21. See also charitable giving
American Civil Liberties Union (ACLU), 83
American Heart Association, 85, 90
Ames, Ruth, 157–58, 176
anabolic steroids, 134, 188–89
Axelrod, Robert, 23, 59

Banfield, Edward, 144
behavior: mechanics of, 14. See also human motivation
Ben & Jerry's, 66
Bentham, Jeremy, 48
Body Shop, The, 66
bonding: mimicry and, 16–17; physical proximity and, 17–18
Brammer, G., 99
Brewster, Daniel, 85
Bush, George W. (President), 186, 189

career choice: moral satisfaction and, 72–75; and recruitment by socially responsible firms, 66–67. See also wage differentials
career lock-in, 61–62
Carr, Albert, 67–68
Carter, John, 158–60, 176

Cellucci, Anthony, 74
Chammah, A., 23
character judgments, bases for, 10
Chariots of Fire, 144
charitable giving: the cause, centrality of, 121; by economists, 160–65; framing of appeals for, 126–29; and moral sentiments, appeals to, 121–26; motives for, 112–14; and multiple motives, strategic problem of appealing to, 119–21; the rational actor model and the understanding of, 110, 129–30; self-interested reasons for, 161
Cleese, John, 109–11
cognition: framing effects and, 115–18, 126–29; psychophysics of perception and, 118–19
Coleman, James, 141–42
commitment: contractual, 5–8, 62; devices, 4–5; emotional, 5–8, 183–84; problems of, 52, 60–65; sympathy and, 19 (see also sympathy). See also cooperation
communication: role of in cooperation, 31. See also experiment in cooperation
compensation: breakdown of social norms and, 153. See also wages
competition, socially responsible firms and. See socially responsible firms
confidentiality, 64–65
consequentialist moral theory, 55–56
conspicuous consumption, 139–41, 144
consumption: absolute *vs.* relative forms of, 185; conspicuous mode of, 139–41, 144
contractual commitments, 5–8, 62
cooperation: communication and, 31; and complications in modeling, 13; of cooperators and defectors, problem of, 8–10; by economists (see economists); of firms in one-shot dilemmas (see socially respon-